Wild Strawberries

INGMAR BERGMAN

Translated from the Swedish by
LARS MALMSTRÖM AND DAVID KUSHNER

faber and faber
LONDON · BOSTON

First published in Great Britain in 1986 by Lorrimer Publishing Limited
This edition published in 1993 by Faber and Faber Limited
3 Queen Square London WCIN 3AU

Printed in England by Clays Ltd, St Ives plc

Original Swedish language film entitled *Smultronstället* by Ingmar Bergman
© 1957
English translation © by Ingmar Bergman, 1960
This edition © Faber and Faber, 1993

A CIP record for this book is
available from the British Library

ISBN 0–571–12652–9

2 4 6 8 10 9 7 5 3 1

CONTENTS

ACKNOWLEDGMENTS

The publishers wish to express their gratitude for the help and co-operation received from the staff of Janus Films, Inc., particularly Cyrus Harvey, Jr.

The English translation of Ingmar Bergman's tribute to Victor Sjöström appeared in *Sight and Sound*, Spring 1960.

A NOTE ON THIS EDITION

In our series of Classic and Modern Film Scripts, we hope that *Wild Strawberries* will serve as a precise example of how a literary script is translated into visual terms. The literary script in this book is identical to that used by Ingmar Bergman when filming, except that: (1) the original script contained numbers before each sequence indicating the estimated number of shots which would be necessary for that sequence; (2) since this script was prepared before shooting began, it contains sequences and dialogue which do not appear in the final film. Bergman has deleted some material to make the published script conform to the film; other important alterations and additions are indicated in the script by footnotes and square brackets. The script in itself amply conveys the continuity of the film by its sheer literary quality. However, it contains no technical details of camera position and movement, and for this reason a shot-by-shot cutting continuity is included in this edition which, together with the stills keyed to the text, should help the reader to visualise the action. In this cutting continuity, the camera position is indicated by initials: CU for close-up; MCU for medium close-up; MS for medium shot; MLS for medium long shot; LS for long shot.

BERGMAN DISCUSSES FILM-MAKING

My association with film goes back to the world of child-hood.

My grandmother had a very large old apartment in Uppsala. I used to sit under the dining-room table there, ' listening ' to the sunshine which came in through the gigantic windows. The cathedral bells went ding-dong, and the sunlight moved about and ' sounded ' in a special way. One day, when winter was giving way to spring and I was five years old, a piano was being played in the next apartment.It played waltzes, nothing but waltzes. On the wall hung a large picture of Venice. As the sunlight moved across the picture the water in the canal began to flow, the pigeons flew up from the square, people talked and gesticulated. Bells sounded, not those of Uppsala Cathedral but from the picture itself. And the piano music also came from that remarkable picture of Venice.

A child who is born and brought up in a vicarage acquires an early familiarity with life and death behind the scenes. Father performed funerals, marriages, baptisms, gave advice and prepared sermons. The devil was an early acquaintance, and in the child's mind there was a need to personify him. This is where my magic lantern came in. It consisted of a small metal box with a carbide lamp — I can still remember the smell of the hot metal — and coloured glass slides : Red Riding Hood and the Wolf, and all the others. And the Wolf was the Devil, without horns but with a tail and a gaping red mouth, strangely real yet incomprehensible, a picture of wickedness and temptation on the flowered wall of the nursery.

When I was ten years old I received my first, rattling film projector, with its chimney and lamp. I found it both mystifying and fascinating. The first film I had was nine feet long and brown in colour. It showed a girl lying asleep in a meadow, who woke up and stretched out her arms, then disappeared to the right. That was all there was to it. The film was a great success and was projected every night until it broke and could not be mended any more.

This little rickety machine was my first conjuring set. And even today I remind myself with childish excitement that I am really a conjurer, since cinematography is based on deception of the human eye. I have worked it out that if I see a film which has a running time of one hour, I sit through twenty-seven minutes of complete darkness — the blankness between frames. When I show a film I am guilty of deceit. I use an apparatus which is constructed to take advantage of a certain human weakness, an apparatus with which I can sway my audience in a highly emotional manner—make them laugh, scream with fright, smile, believe in fairy stories, become indignant, feel shocked, charmed, deeply moved or perhaps yawn with boredom. Thus I am either an imposter or, when the audience is willing to be taken in, a conjurer. I perform conjuring tricks with apparatus so expensive and so wonderful that any entertainer in history would have given anything to have it.

A film for me begins with something very vague — a chance remark or a bit of conversation, a hazy but agreeable event unrelated to any particular situation. It can be a few bars of music, a shaft of light across the street. Sometimes in my work at the theatre I have envisioned actors made up for yet unplayed roles.

These are split second impressions that disappear as quickly as they come, yet leave behind a mood — like pleasant dreams. It is a mental state, not an actual story, but one abounding in fertile associations and images. Most of all, it is a brightly coloured thread sticking out of the dark sack of the unconscious. If I begin to wind up this thread, and do it carefully, a complete film will emerge.

This primitive nucleus strives to achieve definite form, moving in a way that may be lazy and half asleep at first. Its stirring is accompanied by vibrations and rhythms which are very special and unique to each film. The picture sequences then assume a pattern in accordance with these rhythms, obeying laws born out of and conditioned by my original stimulus.

7

If that embryonic substance seems to have enough strength to be made into a film, I decide to materialize it. Then comes something very complicated and difficult: the transformation of rhythms, moods, atmosphere, tensions, sequences, tones and scents into words and sentences, into an understandable screenplay.

This is an almost impossible task.

The only thing that can be satisfactorily transferred from that original complex of rhythms and moods is the dialogue, and even dialogue is a sensitive substance which may offer resistance. Written dialogue is like a musical score, almost incomprehensible to the average person. Its interpretation demands a technical knack plus a certain kind of imagination and feeling — qualities which are so often lacking, even among actors. One can write dialogue, but how it should be delivered, its rhythm and tempo, what is to take place between lines — all this must be omitted for practical reasons. Such a detailed script would be unreadable. I try to squeeze instructions as to location, characterisation and atmosphere into my screenplays in understandable terms, but the success of this depends on my writing ability and the perceptiveness of the reader, which are not always predictable.

Now we come to essentials, by which I mean montage, rhythm and the relation of one picture to another—the vital third dimension without which the film is merely a dead product from a factory. Here I cannot clearly give a key, as in a musical score, nor a specific idea of the tempo which determines the relationship of the elements involved. It is quite impossible for me to indicate the way in which the film ' breathes ' and pulsates.

I have often wished for a kind of notation which would enable me to put on paper all the shades and tones of my vision, to record distinctly the inner structure of a film. For when I stand in the artistically devastating atmosphere of the studio, my hands and head full of all the trivial and irritating details that go with motion-picture production, it often takes a tremendous effort to remember how I originally saw and thought out this or that sequence, or what was the relation between the scene of four weeks ago and that of today. If I could express myself clearly, in explicit symbols, then this problem would be almost eliminated and I could work with absolute confidence that whenever I liked I could prove the relationship between the part and the whole and put my finger on the rhythm, the continuity of the film.

Thus the script is a very imperfect *technical* basis for a film. And there is another important point in this connection which I should like to mention. Film has nothing to do with literature; the character and substance of the two art forms are usually in conflict. This probably has something to do with the receptive process of the mind. The written word is read and assimilated by a conscious act of the will in alliance with the intellect; little by little it affects the imagination and the emotions. The process is different with a motion picture. When we experience a film, we consciously prime ourselves for illusion. Putting aside will and intellect, we make way for it in our imagination. The sequence of pictures plays directly on our feelings.

Music works in the same fashion; I would say that there is no art form that has so much in common with film as music. Both affect our emotions directly, not via the intellect. And film is mainly rhythm; it is inhalation and exhalation in continuous sequence. Ever since childhood, music has been my great source of recreation and stimulation, and I often experience a film or play musically.

It is mainly because of this difference between film and literature that we should avoid making films out of books. The irrational dimension of a literary work, the germ of its existence, is often untranslatable into visual terms — and it, in turn, destroys the special, irrational dimension of the film. If, despite this, we wish to translate something literary into film terms, we must make an infinite number of complicated adjustments which often bear little or no fruit in proportion to the effort expended.

I myself have never had any ambition to be an author. I do not want to write novels, short stories, essays, biographies, or even plays for the theatre. I only want to make films — films about conditions, tensions, pictures, rhythms and characters which are in one way or another important to

9

me. The motion picture, with its complicated process of birth, is my method of saying what I want to my fellow men. I am a film-maker, not an author.

Thus the writing of the script is a difficult period but a useful one, for it compels me to prove logically the validity of my ideas. In doing this, I am caught in a conflict — a conflict between my need to transmit a complicated situation through visual images, and my desire for absolute clarity. I do not intend my work to be solely for the benefit of myself or the few, but for the entertainment of the general public. The wishes of the public are imperative. But sometimes I risk following my own impulse, and it has been shown that the public can respond with surprising sensitivity to the most unconventional line of development.

When shooting begins, the most important thing is that those who work with me feel a definite contact, that all of us somehow cancel out our conflicts through working together. We must pull in one direction for the sake of the work at hand. Sometimes this leads to dispute, but the more definite and clear the 'marching orders,' the easier it is to reach the goal which has been set. This is the basis for my conduct as a director, and perhaps the explanation of much of the nonsense that has been written about me.

While I cannot let myself be concerned with what people think and say about me personally, I believe that reviewers and critics have every right to interpret my films as they like. I refuse to interpret my work to others, and I cannot tell the critic what to think; each person has the right to understand a film as he sees it. Either he is attracted or repelled. A film is made to create reaction. If the audience does not react one way or another, it is an indifferent work and worthless.

I do not mean by this that I believe in being 'different' at any price. A lot has been said about the value of originality, and I find this foolish. Either you are original or you are not. It is completely natural for artists to take from and give to each other, to borrow from and experience one another. In my own life, my great literary experience was Strindberg. There are works of his which can still make my hair stand on end — *The People of Hemsö*, for example. And it is my dream to produce *Dream Play* some day. Olof Molander's production of it in 1934 was for me a fundamental dramatic experience.

On a personal level, there are many people who have meant a great deal to me. My father and mother were certainly of vital importance, not only in themselves but because they created a world for me to revolt against. In my family there was an atmosphere of hearty wholesomeness which I, a sensitive young plant, scorned and rebelled against. But that strict middle-class home gave me a wall to pound on, something to sharpen myself against. At the same time they taught me a number of values — efficiency, punctuality, a sense of financial responsibility — which may be ' bourgeois ' but are nevertheless important to the artist. They are part of the process of setting oneself severe standards. Today as a film-maker I am conscientious, hard-working and extremely careful; my films involve good craftsmanship, and my pride is the pride of a good craftsman.

Among the people who have meant something in my professional development is Torsten Hammaren of Gothenburg. I went there from Hälsingborg, where I had been head of the municipal theatre for two years. I had no conception of what theatre was; Hammaren taught me during the four years I stayed in Gothenburg. Then, when I made my first attempts at film, Alf Sjöberg — who directed *Torment* — taught me a great deal. And there was Lorens Marmstedt, who really taught me film-making from scratch after my first unsuccessful movie. Among other things I learned from Marmstedt is the one unbreakable rule : you must look at your own work very coldly and clearly; you must be a devil to yourself in the screening room when watching the day's rushes. Then there is Herbert Grevenius, one of the few who believed in me as a writer. I had trouble with script-writing, and was reaching out more and more to the drama, to dialogue, as a means of expression. He gave me great encouragement.

Finally, there is Carl Anders Dymling, my producer. He is crazy enough to place more faith in the sense of responsibility

11

of a creative artist than in calculations of profit and loss. I am thus able to work with an integrity that has become the very air I breathe, and one of the main reasons I do not want to work outside of Sweden. The moment I lose this freedom I will cease to be a film-maker, because I have no skill in the art of compromise. My only significance in the world of film lies in the freedom of my creativity.

Today, the ambitious film-maker is obliged to walk a tightrope without a net. He may be a conjurer, but no one conjures the producer, the bank director or the theatre owners when the public refuses to go to see a film and lay down the money by which producer, bank director, theatre owner and conjurer can live. The conjurer may then be deprived of his magic wand; I would like to be able to measure the amount of talent, initiative and creative ability which has been destroyed by the film industry in its ruthlessly efficient sausage machine. What was play to me once has now become a struggle. Failure, criticism, public indifference all hurt more today than yesterday. The brutality of the industry is undisguised — yet that can be an advantage.

So much for people and the film business. I have been asked, as a clergyman's son, about the role of religion in my thinking and film-making. To me, religious problems are continuously alive. I never cease to concern myself with them; it goes on every hour of every day. Yet this does not take place on the emotional level, but on an intellectual one. Religious emotion, religious sentimentality, is something I got rid of long ago — I hope. The religious problem is an intellectual one to me : the relationship of my mind to my intuition. The result of this conflict is usually some kind of tower of Babel.

Philosophically, there is a book which was a tremendous experience for me : Eiono Kaila's *Psychology of the Personality*. His thesis that man lives strictly according to his needs — negative and positive — was shattering to me, but terribly true. And I built on this ground.

INGMAR BERGMAN

12

TRIBUTE TO VICTOR SJOSTROM

On the 20th of February, 1960 Ingmar Bergman delivered an address at the Swedish Film Academy. The following tribute to Victor Sjöström is a slightly abridged translation of that address.

No. I can't compose a speech in memory of Victor Sjöström. I suspect he would smile with the utmost irony if he could see me making such a speech.

Instead, I shall simply pass on a few brief impressions — jottings set down in my notebook while we were actually filming *Wild Strawberries*. They are very personal lines my pencil has drawn. But for me they are like engravings, and very much alive.

What I and the rest of us in the team who were filming at that time witnessed was the struggle of a tremendous will against the forces of annihilation. From moment to moment the struggle raged on, with victories and defeats equal on either side.

But when the film was finished and the artist no longer had a strict working routine, like a bulwark, to protect him, the enemy took a merciless revenge and plunged him into nameless suffering. His soul tried in vain to ward off the threat of refrigeration, extinction. The prison walls of his chosen isolation became thicker and thicker all around him . . . It was a cruelly tortured prisoner who was finally given his freedom.

I read a few lines from my diary :

' I can't rid myself of the notion that this old man is a child who has aged in some extraordinary way, having at birth been deprived of both parents and brothers or sisters; a child who is endlessly searching for a security that is just as endlessly denied him.

' It's for this reason he almost brutally rejects all affection that isn't sincere. He loathes it when people stretch out their soft, sticky fingers to catch him, and he spits on all half-

13

hearted or self-seeking sympathy. Even so . . .

' In his mind's despairing duality he does not succeed in hiding or keeping secret his pain. In front of everyone who stands near him he shows his always infected, always open bleeding sore.

' The death of his wife . . .

' Ceaselessly he repeats his accusations against an unjust god who obliterated the only comforting reality he had and who cast him out into the waste land.

' His glance is for ever trying to pierce through the darkness. He is for ever trying to catch the sound of a reply to his terrified questions and despairing prayers. But the silence is complete.'

Another page from my diary :

' I never stop pryingly, shamelessly studying this powerful face. Sometimes it is like a dumb cry of pain, sometimes it is distorted by mistrustful cruelty and senile querulousness, sometimes it dissolves into self-pity and astoundingly senti-mental effusions.

' But there are also other moments which I shall never forget.

' Suddenly he can turn toward us with a smile, a gesture of spontaneous tenderness, his tone of voice expressing a subtle wisdom. At such times it becomes no effort at all for us to love him and we can meet him simply and in the sunniest concord.'

A third jotting from my diary :

' We have shot our final supplementary scenes of *Wild Strawberries* — the final close-ups of Isak Borg as he is brought to clarity and reconciliation. His face shone with secretive light, as if reflected from another reality. His features became suddenly mild, almost effete. His look was open, smiling, tender.

' It was like a miracle.

' Then complete stillness — peace and clarity of soul. Never before or since have I experienced a face so noble and liberated.

' Yet it was all nothing more than a piece of acting in a dirty studio. And acting it had to be. This exceedingly shy

14

human being would never have shown us lookers-on this deeply buried treasure of sensitive purity, if it had not been in a piece of acting; in simulation . . .

'In the presence of this face I recalled the final words of Strindberg's last drama *The Great Highway*: the prayer to a god somewhere in the darkness.

" Bless me, Thy humanity
That suffers, suffers from Thy gift of life!
Me first, who most have suffered —
Suffered most the pain of not being what I most would be." '

INGMAR BERGMAN

CREDITS:

Swedish title	Smultronstället
Screenplay	Ingmar Bergman
Director	Ingmar Bergman
Assistant director	Gösta Ekman
Director of photography	Gunnar Fischer
Assistant cameraman	Björn Thermenius
Music	Erik Nordgren
Music directed by	E. Eckert-Lundin
Sets	Gittan Gustafsson
Costumes	Millie Ström
Make-up	Nils Nittel (of Carl M. Lundh, Inc.)
Sound	Aaby Wedin and Lennart Wallin
Editor	Oscar Rosander
Production supervisor	Allan Ekelund
Produced by	Svensk Filmindustri
Distributed by	Janus Films Inc., in the United States, and by Gala Films Ltd., in Great Britain
Running time	90 minutes

Professor Isak Borg	Victor Sjöström
Sara	Bibi Andersson
Marianne	Ingrid Thulin
Evald	Gunnar Björnstrand
Agda	Jullan Kindahl
Anders	Folke Sundquist
Viktor	Björn Bjelvenstam
Isak's mother	Naima Wifstrand
Mrs. Alman	Gunnel Broström
Isak's wife	Gertrud Fridh
Her lover	Ake Fridell
Aunt	Sif Ruud
Alman	Gunnar Sjöberg
Akerman	Max von Sydow
Uncle Aron	Yngve Nordwald
Sigfrid	Per Sjöstrand
Sigbritt	Gio Petré
Charlotta	Gunnel Lindblom
Angelica	Maud Hansson
Mrs. Akerman	Anne-Mari Wiman
Anna	Eva Norée
The twins	Lena Bergman and Monica Ehrling
Hagbart	Per Skogsberg
Benjamin	Göran Lundquist
Promoter	Professor Helge Wulff

NOTE: *There are no cast listings for Tiger and Jakob because the scene in which these characters appear (see pp. 88-89) did not appear in the finished film.*

WILD STRAWBERRIES

[*At the age of seventy-six, I feel that I'm much too old to lie to myself. But, of course, I can't be too sure. My complacent attitude towards my own truthfulness could be dishonesty in disguise, although I don't quite know what I might want to hide. Nevertheless, if for some reason I would have to evaluate myself, I am sure that I would do so without shame or concern for my reputation. But if I should be asked to express an opinion about someone else, I would be considerably more cautious. There is the greatest danger in passing such judgment. In all probability one is guilty of errors, exaggerations, even tremendous lies. Rather than commit such follies, I remain silent.*

As a result, I have of my own free will withdrawn almost completely from society, because one's relationship with other people consists mainly of discussing and evaluating one's neighbour's conduct. Therefore I have found myself rather alone in my old age. This is not a regret but a statement of fact. All I ask of life is to be left alone and to have the opportunity to devote myself to the few things which continue to interest me, however superficial they may be. For example, I derive pleasure from keeping up with the steady progress made in my profession (I once taught bacteriology), I find relaxation in a game of golf, and now and then I read some memoirs or a good detective story.

My life has been filled with work, and for that I am grateful. It began with a struggle for daily bread and developed into the continuous pursuit of a beloved science. I have a son living in Lund who is a physician and has been married for many years. He has no children. My mother is still living and quite active despite her advanced age (she is ninety-six). She lives in the vicinity of Huskvarna. We seldom see each other.

My nine sisters and brothers are dead, but they left a number of children and grandchildren. I have very little contact with my relatives. My wife Karin died many years ago. Our marriage was quite unhappy. I am fortunate in having a good housekeeper.

That is all I have to say about myself. Perhaps I ought to add that I am an old pedant, and at times quite trying, both to myself and to the people who have to be around me. I detest emotional outbursts, women's tears and the crying of children. On the whole, I find loud noises and sudden startling occurrences most disconcerting.

Later I will come back to the reason for writing this story, which is, as nearly as I can make it, a true account of the events, dreams and thoughts which befell me on a certain day.]* (Stills on page 17)

In the early morning of Saturday, the first of June, I had a strange and very unpleasant dream. I dreamed that I was taking my usual morning stroll through the streets. It was quite early and no human being was in sight. This was a bit surprising to me. I also noted that there were no vehicles parked along the kerbs. The city seemed strangely deserted, as if it were a holiday morning in the middle of summer.

The sun was shining brightly and made sharp black shadows, but it gave off no warmth. Even though I walked on the sunny side, I felt chilly.

The stillness was also remarkable. I usually stroll along a broad, tree-lined boulevard, and even before sunrise the sparrows and crows are as a rule extremely noisy. Besides, there is always the perpetual roar from the centre of the city. But this morning nothing was heard, the silence was absolute, and my footsteps echoed almost anxiously against the walls of the buildings. I began to wonder what had happened.

Just at that moment I passed the shop of a watchmaker-

---

* In the film, the scene in square brackets appears before the credits against shots of Isak in the library.

*optometrist, whose sign had always been a large clock
that gave the exact time. Under this clock hung a
picture of a pair of giant eyeglasses with staring eyes.
On my morning walks I had always smiled to myself
at this slightly grotesque detail in the street scene.*

*To my amazement, the hands of the clock had dis-
appeared. The dial was blank, and below it someone
had smashed both of the eyes so that they looked like
watery, infected sores. (Still on page 18)*

*Instinctively I pulled out my own watch to check the
time, but I found that my old reliable gold timepiece
had also lost its hands. I held it to my ear to find out if
it was still ticking. Then I heard my heart beat. It was
pounding very fast and irregularly. I was overwhelmed
by an inexplicable feeling of frenzy.*

*I put my watch away and leaned for a few moments
against the wall of a building until the feeling had passed.
My heart calmed down and I decided to return home.*

*To my joy, I saw that someone was standing on the
street corner. His back was towards me. I rushed up to
him and touched his arm. (Still on page 18) He turned
quickly and to my horror I found that the man had no
face under his soft felt hat. (Still on page 18)*

*I pulled my hand back (Still on page 18) and in the
same moment the entire figure collapsed as if it were
made of dust or frail splinters. (Still on page 18) On
the sidewalk lay a pile of clothes. The person himself
had disappeared without a trace. I looked around in
bewilderment and realized that I must have lost my
way. I was in a part of the city where I had never been
before. (Still on page 18)*

*I stood on an open square surrounded by high, ugly
apartment buildings. From this narrow square, streets
spread out in all directions. Everyone was dead; there
was not a sign of a living soul.*

*High above me the sun shone completely white, and
light forced its way down between the houses as if it were
the blade of a razor-sharp knife. I was so cold that my
entire body shivered.*

25

Finally I found the strength to move again and chose one of the narrow streets at random. I walked as quickly as my pounding heart allowed, yet the street seemed to be endless.

Then I heard the tolling of bells and suddenly I was standing on another open square near an unattractive little church of red brick. There was no graveyard next to it and the church was surrounded on all sides by grey-walled buildings.

Not far from the church a funeral procession was wending its way slowly through the streets, led by an ancient hearse and followed by some old-fashioned hired carriages. These were pulled by pairs of meagre-looking horses, weighed down under enormous black shabracks. I stopped and uncovered my head. It was an intense relief to see living creatures, hear the sound of horses trotting and church bells ringing. Then everything happened very quickly and so frighteningly that even as I write this I still feel a definite uneasiness. *(Still on page 18)*

The hearse was just about to turn in front of the church gate when suddenly it began to sway and rock like a ship in a storm. I saw that one of the wheels had come loose and was rolling towards me with a loud clatter. I had to throw myself to one side to avoid being hit. It struck the church wall right behind me and splintered into pieces. *(Still on page 19)*

The other carriages stopped at a distance but no one got out or came to help. The huge hearse swayed and teetered on its three wheels. Suddenly the coffin was thrown out and fell into the street. As if relieved, the hearse straightened and rolled on towards a side street, followed by the other carriages. *(Still on page 19)*

The tolling of the church bells had stopped and I stood alone with the overturned, partly smashed coffin. Gripped by a fearful curiosity, I approached. A hand stuck out from the pile of splintered boards. *(Still on page 19)*

When I leaned forward, the dead hand clutched my arm and pulled me down towards the casket with enormous *force. (Still on page 19) I struggled helplessly against it as the corpse slowly rose from the coffin. It was a man dressed in a frock coat.*

To my horror, I saw that the corpse was myself. I tried to free my arm, but he held it in a powerful grip. All this time he stared at me without emotion and seemed to be smiling scornfully. (Still on page 19)

In this moment of senseless horror, I awakened and sat up in my bed. It was three in the morning and the sun was already reflecting from the rooftops opposite my window. I closed my eyes and I muttered words of reality against my dream — against all the evil and frightening dreams which have haunted me these last few years.

ISAK : My name is Isak Borg. I am still alive. I am seventy-six years old.* I really feel quite well.

When I had muttered these words I felt calmer, drank a glass of water, and lay down to ponder on the day which was ahead of me. I knew immediately what I should do. I got out of bed, pulled open the curtains, found the weather radiant, and breathed in the fine morning air. Then I put on my robe and went through the apartment (where the clocks were striking three) to the room of my old housekeeper. When I opened the door she sat up immediately, wide awake.

AGDA : Are you ill, Professor? *(Still on page 20)*

ISAK : Listen, Miss Agda, will you please prepare some breakfast? I'm taking the car.

AGDA : You're taking the car, Professor?

ISAK : Yes, I'll drive down to Lund with my own two hands. I've never believed in aeroplanes.

AGDA : Dear Professor! Go back to sleep and I'll bring you coffee at nine o'clock and then we'll start at ten, as was decided.

ISAK : Very well then, I'll go without eating.

AGDA : And who's going to pack the frock coat?

ISAK : I'll do that myself. *(Still on page 20)*

AGDA : And what will become of me?

---

* In the film, Isak is seventy-eight.

ISAK : Miss Agda, you can go with me in the car or take the aeroplane — that's up to you.

AGDA : For an entire year I've been looking forward to being present at the ceremony when you become a Jubilee Doctor, and everything was perfectly organised. Now you come and tell me that you're going to drive down instead of going by plane.

ISAK : The presentation is not until five o'clock, and if I leave at once I'll have fourteen hours in which to get there.

AGDA : Everything will be ruined that way. Your son will be waiting at Malmö airport. What will he say?

ISAK : You can make some explanation, Miss Agda.

AGDA : If you take the car, I won't be with you at the ceremony.

ISAK : Now listen, Miss Agda.

AGDA : You can take the car and drive there and destroy the most solemn day of my life . . .

ISAK : We are not married, Miss Agda.

AGDA : I thank God every night that we're not. For seventy-four years I have acted according to my own principles, and they won't fail me today.

ISAK : Is that your last word on this matter, Miss Agda?

AGDA : That is my last word. But I'll be saying a lot to myself about mean old gentlemen who think only of themselves and never about the feelings of others who have served them faithfully for forty years.

ISAK : I really don't know how I've been able to stand your immense hunger for power all these years.

AGDA : Just tell me and it can be ended tomorrow.

ISAK : Anyway, I'm going to drive, and you may do whatever the hell you want to. I'm a grown man and I don't have to put up with your bossiness.

Our last words, I must admit, were spoken rather loudly, partly because of Miss AGDA's unruly temper and partly because I had gone to the bathroom, where I shaved and completed my morning toilet. When I came out of the bathroom, I found to my surprise that Miss AGDA was busy packing my frock coat and other necessities. She seemed to have come to her senses and I tried a friendly

28

*pat on her back to make her understand that I had
forgiven her.*

ISAK : There is no one who can pack like you.

AGDA : Is that so.

ISAK : Old sourpuss.

*I was very angry that she didn't answer. True, my last
words weren't very well chosen, but Miss AGDA has a way
of being cross which would try the patience of a saint.*

AGDA : Should I boil a couple of eggs to go with the coffee,
sir?

ISAK : Yes, thank you, that's very kind of you, Miss Agda.
Thank you, dear Miss Agda.

*Without noticing my efforts to be nice in spite of every-
thing, the old lady disappeared into the kitchen.*

ISAK : Jubilee Doctor! Damn stupidity. The faculty could just
as well make me jubilee idiot. I'm going to buy something for
the old sourpuss to sweeten her up a little. I hate people who
are slow to forget. I can't even hurt a fly; how could I ever
hurt Miss Agda?

Then she appeared in the doorway.

AGDA : Do you want toast?

ISAK : No, thank you for everything. Don't trouble yourself
over me.

AGDA : Why are *you* sour?

*I didn't have time to answer before the door closed in
my face. I dressed and went into the dining-room, where
my breakfast was waiting. The morning sun threw a
bright stripe across the dining-room table. Miss AGDA
puttered about quietly with a coffee pot and poured
steaming coffee into my personal cup. (Still on page 20)*

ISAK : Won't you have a cup too?

AGDA : No, thanks.

*Miss AGDA went over to water the flowers in the window
and turned her back to me quite naturally but in a very
definite way. Then the door of a nearby room opened
and my daughter-in-law, MARIANNE, entered. She was
still wearing pyjamas and was smoking a cigarette. (Still
on page 20)*

ISAK : May I ask why my esteemed daughter-in-law is out

of bed at this hour of the morning?

MARIANNE: It's a little difficult to sleep when you and Miss Agda are shouting at each other loud enough to shake the walls.

ISAK: Surely no one here has been shouting.

AGDA: Of course not, no one here has been shouting.

MARIANNE: You're going by car to Lund.

ISAK: Yes, I think so.

MARIANNE: May I go with you?

ISAK: What? You want to go home?

MARIANNE: Yes, I want to go home.

ISAK: Home to Evald?

MARIANNE: That's it. You don't have to ask my reasons. If I could afford it, I would take the train.

ISAK: Of course you can go with me.

MARIANNE: I'll be ready in about ten minutes.

> MARIANNE *put out her cigarette in an ash tray on the table, went into her room and closed the door.* AGDA *brought another cup but said nothing. We were both surprised but had to remain silent about* MARIANNE's *sudden decision to go home to my son* EVALD. *Nevertheless, I felt obliged to shake my head.*

AGDA: Good Lord!

> [*Shortly after half past three, I drove my car out of the garage.* MARIANNE *came out through the front gate dressed in slacks and a short jacket (she is a stately young woman). I looked up towards the window to see if* AGDA *was standing there. She was. I waved to her but she did not wave back. Angrily I got into the car, slammed the door and started the engine.*]* *Silently we left the quiet, sleeping city. (Still on page 20)* MARIANNE *was about to light a cigarette.*

ISAK: Please don't smoke.

MARIANNE: Of course.

ISAK: I can't stand cigarette smoke.

MARIANNE: I forgot.

ISAK: Besides, cigarette smoking is both expensive and un-

---

* The scene in square brackets does not appear in the finished film.

healthy. There should be a law against women smoking.

MARIANNE : The weather is nice.

ISAK : Yes, but oppressive. I have a feeling that we'll have a storm.

MARIANNE : So do I.

ISAK : Now take the cigar. Cigars are an expression of the fundamental idea of smoking. A stimulant and a relaxation. A manly vice.

MARIANNE : And what vices may a woman have?

ISAK : Crying, bearing children, and gossiping about the neighbours.

MARIANNE : How old are you really, Father Isak?

ISAK : Why do you want to know?

MARIANNE : No real reason. Why?

ISAK : I know why you asked.

MARIANNE : Oh.

ISAK : Don't pretend. You don't like me and you never have.

MARIANNE : I know you only as a father-in-law.

ISAK : Why are you going home again?

MARIANNE : An impulse. That's all.

ISAK : Evald happens to be my son.

MARIANNE : Yes, I'm sure he is.

ISAK : So, it may not be so strange that I ask you.

MARIANNE : This is something which really does not concern you.

ISAK : Do you want to hear my opinion?

She provoked me with her unshakable calm and remoteness. Besides, I was very curious and a little worried.

ISAK : Evald and I are very much alike. We have our principles.

MARIANNE : You don't have to tell me.

ISAK : This *loan* for example. Evald got a loan from me with which to complete his studies. He was to have paid it back when he became a lecturer at the university. It became a matter of honour for him to pay it back at the rate of five thousand per year. Although I realise that it's difficult for him, a bargain is a bargain.

MARIANNE : For us it means that we can never have a holiday together and that your son works himself to death.

31

ISAK : You have an income of your own.

MARIANNE : . . . Especially when you're stinking rich and have no need for the money.

ISAK : A bargain is a bargain, my dear Marianne. And I know that Evald understands and respects me.

MARIANNE : That may be true, but he also hates you.

Her calm, almost matter-of-fact tone startled me. I tried to look into her eyes, but she stared straight ahead and her face remained expressionless.

ISAK : Evald and I have never coddled each other.

MARIANNE : I believe you.

ISAK : I'm sorry that you dislike me, because I rather like you.

MARIANNE : That's nice.

ISAK : Tell me, what do you really have against me?

MARIANNE : Do you want me to be frank?

ISAK : Please.

MARIANNE : You are an old egotist, Father. You are completely inconsiderate and you have never listened to anyone but yourself. All this is well hidden behind your mask of old-fashioned charm and your friendliness. But you are hard as nails, even though everyone depicts you as a great humanitarian. We who have seen you at close range, we know what you really are. You can't fool us. For instance, do you remember when I came to you a month ago? I had some idiotic idea that you would help Evald and me. So I asked to stay with you for a few weeks. Do you remember what you said?

ISAK : I told you that you were most cordially welcome.

MARIANNE : This is what you really said, but I'm sure you've forgotten : Don't try to pull me into your marital problems because I don't give a damn about them, and everyone has his own troubles.

ISAK : Did I say that?

MARIANNE : You said more than that.

ISAK : That was the worst, I hope.

MARIANNE : This is what you said, word for word : I have no respect for suffering of the soul, so don't come to me and complain. But if you need spiritual masturbation, I can make an appointment for you with some good quack, or perhaps with a minister, it's so popular these days.

ISAK : Did I say that?

MARIANNE : You have rather inflexible opinions, Father. It would be terrible to have to depend on you in any way.

ISAK : Is that so. Now, if I am honest, I must say that I've enjoyed having you around the house.

MARIANNE : Like a cat.

ISAK : Like a cat, or a human being, it's the same thing. You are a fine young woman and I'm sorry that you dislike me.

MARIANNE : I don't dislike you.

ISAK : Oh.

MARIANNE : I feel sorry for you.

I could hardly keep from laughing at her odd tone of voice and lack of logic. She herself laughed, by the way, and it cleared the air a bit.

ISAK : I really would like to tell you about a dream I had this morning.

MARIANNE : I'm not very interested in dreams.

ISAK : No, perhaps not.

We drove for a while in silence. The sun stood high in the sky and the road was brilliantly white. Suddenly I had an impulse. I slowed down and swung the car into a small side road on the left, leading down to the sea. It was a twisting, forest road, bordered by piles of newly cut timber which smelled strongly in the heat of the sun. MARIANNE looked up, a bit surprised, but remained silent. I parked the car in a curve of the road. (Still on page 20)

ISAK : Come, I'll show you something.

She sighed quietly and followed me down the little hill to the gate. Now we could see the large yellow house set among the birch trees, with its terrace facing the bay. The house slept behind closed doors and drawn blinds.

ISAK : Every summer for the first twenty years of my life we lived out here. There were ten of us children. Yes, you probably know that. (Still on page 20)*

MARIANNE : What a ridiculous old house.

ISAK : It is an antique.

MARIANNE : Do people live here now?

ISAK : Not this summer.

MARIANNE : I'll go down to the water and take a dip if you don't mind. We have lots of time.

ISAK : I'll go over to the wild strawberry patch for a moment.
I suddenly found that I was speaking without a listener.
MARIANNE *was lazily making her way down to the beach.*

ISAK : The old strawberry patch . . . *(Still on page 20)*

I went towards the house and immediately found the spot, but it seemed to be much smaller and less impressive than I had remembered. There were still many wild straw- berries, however. I sat down next to an old apple tree that stood alone and ate the berries, one by one. I may very well have become a little sentimental. Perhaps I was a little tired and somewhat melancholy. It's not unlikely that I began to think about one thing or another that was associated with my childhood haunts.

I had a strange feeling of solemnity, as if this were a day of decision. (It was not the only time that day that I was to feel that way.) The quietness of the summer morning. The calm bay. The birds' brilliant concert in the foliage. The old sleeping house. The aromatic apple tree which leaned slightly, supporting my back. The wild strawberries.

I don't know how it happened, but the day's clear reality flowed into dreamlike images. I don't even know if it was a dream, or memories which arose with the force of real events. I do not know how it began either, but I think it was when I heard the playing of a piano.

Astonished, I turned my head and looked at the house, a short distance up the hill. It had been transformed in a strange way. The façade, which only a few moments ago was so blind and shut, was now alive and the sun glittered on the open windows. White curtains swayed in the warm summer breeze. The gaudy awnings were rolled halfway down; smoke came from the chimney. The old summer-house seemed to be bursting with life. You could hear the music of the piano (it was something by Waldteufel), happy voices echoing through the open windows, laughter, footsteps, the cries of children, the squeaking of the pump. Someone started to sing up there

34

on the second floor. It was a strong, almost Italian
bel-canto tenor. In spite of all this, not a human being
was in sight. For a few moments the scene still had a
feeling of unreality, like a mirage which could instantly
evaporate and be lost in silence.

Suddenly I saw her. When I turned round after looking
at the strangely transformed house I discovered her
where she was kneeling in her sun-yellow cotton dress,
picking wild strawberries. I recognised her immediately
and I became excited. She was so close to me that I could
touch her, but my lingering feeling of the evanescence of
the situation prevented me from making her notice my
presence. (I was amused. Mental image or dream or
whatever this was, she looked just as I remembered her:
a girl in a yellow summer dress, freckled and tanned and
glowing with light-hearted young womanhood.)

I sat for a few minutes and silently looked at her.
Finally I couldn't help calling out her name, rather
quietly but nevertheless quite audibly. She didn't react. I
tried once more, a little louder. (Still on page 37)

ISAK : Sara . . . It's me, your cousin Isak . . . I've become
a little old, of course, and do not quite look as I used to. But
you haven't changed the slightest bit. Little cousin, can't you
hear me?

She didn't hear me, but eagerly continued to pick the
wild strawberries, putting them into a small straw basket.
(Still on page 37) I understood then that one cannot
easily converse with one's memories. This discovery did
not make me particularly sad. I decided to keep quiet and
hoped that this unusual and pleasant situation would last
as long as possible.

Then, a boy came strolling down the hill. He was
already growing a small moustache despite the fact that
he couldn't have been more than eighteen or nineteen
years old. He was dressed in a shirt and trousers and wore
his student's cap pushed way back on his head. He
stepped right behind SARA, *took off his glasses and wiped*
them with a large white handkerchief. (I recognised him
as my brother SIGFRID, *one year older than myself. We*

35

*shared many happy moments and troubles. He died, by
the way, relatively young, of pyelitis. He was a lecturer
in Slavic languages at Uppsala University.)*

SIGFRID : Good morning, sweet cousin. What are you doing?

SARA : Can't you see that I'm picking wild strawberries,
stupid?

SIGFRID : And who shall be favoured with these tasty berries,
plucked in the morning watch by a dulcet young maiden?

SARA : Oh you! Don't you know that Uncle Aron's birthday
is today? I forgot to prepare a present for him. So, he gets a
basket of wild strawberries. That's good enough, isn't it?

SIGFRID : I'll help you.

SARA : You know, Charlotta and Sigbritt have sewn a sampler
for him and Angelica has baked a cake and Anna has painted
a really pretty picture and Kristina and Birgitta have written
a song which they'll sing.

SIGFRID : That's best of all, because Uncle Aron is stone deaf.

SARA : He will be very happy and you are stupid.

SIGFRID : And the nape of your neck is deuced pretty.

> SIGFRID *quickly bent over the girl and rather gallantly
> kissed her on her downy neck.* SARA *became rather
> annoyed.*

SARA : You know that you're not allowed to do that.

SIGFRID : Who said so?

SARA : I said so. Besides, you are a particularly unbearable
little snot who thinks he's something.

SIGFRID : I'm your cousin, and you're sweet on me.

SARA : On you!

SIGFRID : Come here and I'll kiss you on the mouth.

SARA : If you don't keep away I'll tell Isak that you try to kiss
me all the time.

SIGFRID : Little Isak. I can beat him easily with one hand tied
behind my back.

SARA : Isak and I are secretly engaged. You know that very
well.

SIGFRID : Yes, your engagement is so secret that the whole
house knows about it.

SARA : Could I help it if the twins ran around and blabbered
everything?

SIGFRID : Then when are you going to get married? When are you going to get married? When are you going to get married? When are you going to get married?

SARA : I'll tell you one thing, of your four brothers I can't decide which is the least vain. But I think it's Isak. In any case, he's the kindest. And you are the most awful, the most unbearable, the most stupid, the most idiotic, the most ridiculous, the most cocky — I can't think of enough names to call you.

SIGFRID : Admit that you're a little sweet on me.

SARA : Besides, you smoke smelly cigars.

SIGFRID : That's a man's smell, isn't it?

SARA : Besides, the twins, who know *everything*, say that you've done *rather* nasty things with the oldest Berglund girl. And she's not a *really nice* girl, the twins say. And I believe them.

SIGFRID : If you only knew how pretty you are when you blush like that. Now you must kiss me. I can't stand it any more. I'm completely in love with you, now that I think about it.

SARA : Oh, that's only talk. The twins say that you're crazy about girls. Is it really true?

Suddenly he kissed her hard and rather skilfully. (Still on page 37) She was carried away by this game and returned his kiss with a certain fierceness. But then she was conscious-stricken and threw herself down on the ground, knocking over the basket of wild strawberries. She was very angry and began crying with excitement. (Still on page 37)

SIGFRID : Don't scream. Someone might come.

SARA : Look at the wild strawberries, all spilled. And what will Isak say? He is so kind and really loves me. Oh, how sorry I am, oh, what you've done to me. You've turned me into a bad woman, at least *nearly*. Go away. I don't want to see you any more, at least not before breakfast. I have to hurry. Help me pick up the strawberries. And look, I've got a spot on my dress.

Then the gong suddenly sounded, announcing that breakfast was being served. The sound seemed to bring

41

forth many human beings not far from where I stood, an astonished onlooker.

The flag with the Swedish-Norwegian Union emblem went up and instantly stiffened against the light summer clouds, (Still on page 37) big brother HAGBART, *dressed in his cadet uniform, handled the ropes expertly. (Still on page 37) From the bath-house one could hear wild laughter, and through the louvered door thumbled two redheaded girls about thirteen years old, as identical as two wild strawberries. They laughed so hard they could hardly walk, and they whispered things to each other that were apparently both very secret and quite amusing.* SIGBRITT, *tall and lanky, with thick hair in heavy rolls across her forehead, came out carrying the baby's bassinet and placed it in the shadow of the arbour.* CHARLOTTA *(the diligent, self-sacrificing sister who carried the responsibilities of the household on her round shoulders) rushed out on the veranda and shouted to* SARA *and* SIGFRID *to hurry. Seventeen-year-old* BENJAMIN *dived out of some bushes, his pimply face red from the sun, and looked around with an annoyed expression.* In his hand he held a thick, open book.* ANGELICA *(the beauty of the family) came skipping out of the woods, joined the twins, and was immediately made part of some hilarious secret. Finally, fifteen-year-old* ANNA *came running out of the house, asked* HAGBART *about something, then raised her voice and started to shout for* ISAK.

I arose, surprised and worried, unable to answer her cry.

TWINS *in unison*: I think that Isak is out fishing with Father and they probably can't hear the gong. And Father said, by the way, that we shouldn't wait to eat. That's what Father said, I definitely remember.

Oh, yes, FATHER *and I were out fishing together. I felt a secret and completely inexplicable happiness at this message, and I stood for a long while wondering what I should do in this new old world which I was suddenly*

---

* In the film, Benjamin is seen jumping down from a tree. *(Still on page 37)* *given the opportunity to visit.*

*The rest of the family had entered the house and some-
thing was being discussed quite loudly inside. (Still on
page 37) Only* SIGBRITT's *little child remained on the
terrace, sleeping in the shadows of the tall lilac bushes.
Curiosity overwhelmed me. I went slowly up the slope
towards the house and soon found myself in the long, dark
corridor which was connected with the foyer by glass
doors. From there I had a good view into the large, sunlit
dining-room with its white table already set for breakfast,
the light furniture, the wallpaper, the figurines, the palms,
the airy summer curtains, the scoured white wooden floor
with its broad planks and blue rag rugs, the pictures and
the sampler, the large, crownlike chandelier.*

*There they were now, my nine brothers and sisters,
my aunt and Uncle* ARON. *The only ones missing were*
FATHER, MOTHER *and I.*

*Everyone was standing behind his chair, with lowered
head, and hands clenched together.* AUNT *recited the
prayer ' In Jesus's name to the table we go, Bless You
for the food You bestow.' (Still on page 38) After which
the whole troop sat down with much chatter and scrap-
ing of chairs. (Still on page 38) My aunt (a stately
woman in her best years, endowed with a powerful sense
of authority and a resonant voice) demanded silence.*

AUNT : Benjamin will immediately go and wash his hands.
How long is it going to take you to learn cleanliness?

BENJAMIN : I *have* washed my hands.

AUNT : Sigbritt, pass the porridge to Angelica and give the
twins their portions. Your fingernails are coal-black. Pass me
the bread, Hagbart. Who taught you to spread so much
butter on the bread? Can you do that at the military
academy? Charlotta, the salt-cellar is stopped up. How often
have I told you that it shouldn't be left out in the open,
because the salt gets humid.

BENJAMIN : *I have washed my hands,* but I have paint under
my nails.

UNCLE ARON : Who has picked wild strawberries for me?

SARA : I have. *Louder* : I have.

43

AUNT : You have to speak up, my child. You know that Uncle Aron is a bit hard of hearing.

SARA *thunderously* : *I have* ! *(Still on page 38)*

ARON : Oh my, you remembered Uncle Aron's birthday. That was really very kind of you.

HAGBART : Couldn't Uncle Aron have a little drink for breakfast in honour of the day?

AUNT : A drink at breakfast when Father isn't home is completely out of the question.

TWINS *in unison* : Uncle Aron has already had three drinks. I know. I know. We saw him at eight o'clock when we went down to the bath-house.

AUNT : The twins should hold their tongues and eat. Besides, you haven't made your beds and as punishment you'll have to dry the dinner silverware. Benjamin must not bite his nails. Don't sit and jump on the chair, Anna. You aren't a child any more.

ANNA : I want to give Uncle Aron my picture, please, Auntie. Can't we give him our presents now, right away?

AUNT : Where is your picture?

ANNA : Here under the table.

AUNT : You'll have to wait until we've eaten.

SIGFRID : It's a very advanced work of art, I'd say. It's a picture of Tristan and Isolde, but you can't tell for sure which one is Tristan.

SARA : Oh, he always spoils things, the little fop! Now he's making Anna unhappy. See if she doesn't start to cry.

ANNA : Not at all. I can overlook Sigfrid's faults.

TWINS *together* : By the way, what were Sara and Sigfrid up to in the wild strawberry patch this morning? We saw everything from the bath-house.

SIGBRITT : Calm down now, children !

CHARLOTTA : Someone should put gags on the twins.

AUNT : Twins, keep still or leave the table.

BENJAMIN : Doesn't a person have freedom of expression, eh?

SIGFRID : Shut up, you snotnoses.

ANGELICA : Sara is blushing, Sara is blushing, Sara is blushing.

TWINS : Sigfrid is blushing, too. Ha-ha ! Sigfrid and Sara ! Sigfrid and Sara ! Sigfrid and Sara !

44

AUNT *thunderously*: Quiet! We'll have quiet at the table!

ARON: What did you say? Of course we shall be happy.

> *The* TWINS *snigger in the silence.* SARA *throws the porridge spoon at her tormentors.*

CHARLOTTA: But, Sara!

SARA: They're just lying! They're liars!

> SARA *rose from the table so violently that her chair turned over. She stood hesitantly for a moment, her face red and tears splashing down her cheeks. Then she ran away furiously, throwing herself at the door and out into the hall.*
>
> *She opened the glass door and disappeared out on the porch, where I could hear her sobbing violently. Gentle* CHARLOTTA *came out of the dining-room and went past me on her way to console* SARA. *(Still on page 38)*
>
> *I could hear their voices from the darkness of the foyer and I came closer stealthily.* SARA *sat on a red stool (which* GRANDMOTHER *once used, when she wanted to take off her rubber boots) while* CHARLOTTA *stood in front of her, patting her gently on the head. The miserable girl pressed her tear-stained face against* CHARLOTTA's *skirt over and over again. The tinted light from the stained-glass windows of the outer door painted the whole picture in a strange way. (Still on page 38)*

SARA: Isak is so refined. He is so enormously refined and moral and sensitive and he wants us to read poetry together and he talks about the after-life and wants to play duets on the piano and he likes to kiss only in the dark and he talks about sinfulness. I think he is extremely intellectual and morally aloof and I feel so worthless, and I *am* so worthless, you can't deny that. But sometimes I get the feeling that I'm much older than Isak, do you know what I mean? And then I think he's a child even if we are the same age, and then Sigfrid is so fresh and exciting and I want to go home. I don't want to be here all summer, to be a laughing stock for the twins and the rest of you — *no, I don't want that.*

CHARLOTTA: I'll talk to Sigfrid, I will! If he doesn't leave you alone, I'll see to it that he gets a few more chores to do. Father will arrange that without any trouble. He also thinks Sigfrid

45

is nasty and needs a little work to keep him out of mischief.

SARA : Poor little Isak, he is so kind to me. Oh, how unfair everything is.

CHARLOTTA : Everything will work out for the best, you'll see. Listen, now they're singing for Uncle Aron.

SARA : Isn't it crazy to write a song for a deaf man! That's typical of the twins.

Then two girlish voices sang a song that could be heard throughout the house. CHARLOTTA placed her arm around SARA's shoulders and SARA blew her nose quite loudly. Both girls returned to the dining-room, where the mood had become very lively.* Uncle ARON had arisen, his round perspiring face lit like a lantern, and he had tears in his eyes. He held a sheet of music before him while the twins stood nearby and sang with all their might. (Still on page 38) When they had finished everyone applauded, and Uncle ARON kissed them on the forehead and wiped his face with a napkin. My Aunt rose from the table and proposed a quadruple cheer. Everyone got up and hurrahed. Suddenly ANNA shouted and pointed out the window. Everyone turned to look.

ANNA : Look, here comes Father.

AUNT : Well, finally! Sigbritt, take out the porridge bowl and have it warmed. Charlotta, you bring up more milk from the cellar.

The women fussed around, but SARA ran out of the house, down the slope, and disappeared behind the small arbour which stood on the edge of the birch-tree pasture. I followed her with curiosity, but lost her. Suddenly I stood alone at the wild strawberry patch. A feeling of emptiness and sadness came over me. I was awakened by a girl's voice asking me something. I looked up.

In front of me stood a young lady in shorts and a boy's checked shirt. She was very tanned and her blonde hair was tangled and bleached by the sun and the sea. She sucked on an unlit pipe, wore wooden sandals on her

---

* In the film, the girls do not return to the dining-room. (Still on page 38) *feet and dark glasses on her nose.*

Sara : Is this your shack?

Isak : No, it isn't.

Sara : It's a good thing you're the truthful type. My old man owns the whole peninsula . . . including the shack.

Isak : I lived here once. Two hundred years ago.

Sara : Uh huh. Is that your jalopy standing up at the gate?

Isak : It's my jalopy, yes.

Sara : Looks like an antique.

Isak : It *is* an antique, just like its owner.

Sara : You've got a sense of humour about yourself, too. That's fantastic. Where are you heading, by the way? In which direction, I mean.

Isak : I'm going to Lund.

Sara : What a fantastic coincidence. I'm on my way to Italy.

Isak : I'd feel very honoured if you came along.

Sara : My name is Sara. Silly name, isn't it?

Isak : My name is Isak. Rather silly too.

Sara : Weren't they married?

Isak : Unfortunately not. It was Abraham and Sara.

Sara : Shall we take off?

Isak : I have another lady with me. *(Still on page 38)* Here she comes. This is Sara, and this is Marianne. We'll have company to Lund. Sara is going to Italy but she has agreed to travel part of the way with us.

Sara : Now you're being ironic again, but it suits you.

We began walking towards the car. Marianne *and I exchanged amused glances, the first contact between us. When we came to the car, two young men with round blond crew-cut heads popped up.* They were also wearing checked shirts, shorts, wooden sandals and sunglasses. Each carried a rucksack.*

Sara : Hey, fellows. I've got a lift nearly all the way to Italy. This is Anders, and this one with the glasses is Viktor, called Vicke . . . and this is Father Isak.

Viktor : Hello.

Isak : Hello.

---

* In the film, one of the young men has dark hair.

ANDERS : How do you do, sir.

ISAK : Hello.

SARA : That cookie you're staring at so hard, her name is Marianne.

MARIANNE : Hello.

BOYS *together* : Hello.

SARA : It's a pretty big car.

ISAK : Just jump in. There's room for everybody. We can put the baggage in the boot, if you don't mind.

We packed things away, and then we all got into the car. I drove carefully, leaving my childhood world behind. (Still on page 39) SARA took off her sunglasses and laughed. She was very much like her namesake of the past.

SARA : Of course I have to tell Isak that Anders and I are going steady. We are crazy about each other. Viktor is with us as a chaperon. That was decided by the old man. Viktor is also in love with me and is watching Anders like a madman. This was a brilliant idea of my old man. I'll probably have to seduce Viktor to get him out of the way. I'd better tell Isak that I'm a virgin. That's why I can talk so brazenly.

I looked at her through the rear-view mirror. She was sitting comfortably with her legs on the backs of the folding seats. ANDERS had a proprietary arm around her shoulders and looked rather angry, for which I could hardly blame him. VIKTOR, on the other hand, seemed completely disinterested and stared fixedly at the nape of MARIANNE's neck — and whatever else he could glimpse of her figure.

SARA : I smoke a pipe. Viktor says it's healthier. He's crazy about everything that's healthy.

No one answered, or considered any comment necessary. We continued our trip in a silence which was by no means unpleasant, just a little shy. The weather had become quite warm, almost oppressive, and we had opened all the windows. The road was broad and straight. I was in a spirited mood. The day had been full of stimulating surprises.

ISAK : I had a first love whose name was Sara.

SARA : She was like me, of course.

ISAK : As a matter of fact, she was rather like you.

SARA : What happened to her?

ISAK : She married my brother Sigfrid and had six children. Now she's seventy-five years old and a rather beautiful little old lady.

SARA : I can't imagine anything worse than getting old. Oh, excuse me. I think I said something stupid.

Her tone was so sincerely repentant that everyone burst into laughter. And then it happened.

We were on a broad, blind right curve. I kept hard to the left and at that moment a little black car came speeding straight towards us. (Still on page 39) I had time to see MARIANNE *brace her right hand against the windshield and I heard* SARA *scream. Then I slammed on the brakes with all my strength. Our big car skidded to the left and went off the road into a pasture. The black car disappeared with a squeal, rolled over and fell into a deep ditch to the right of the road. Startled, we stared at one another; we had escaped without a scratch. Some thick black tyre tracks and several big marks on the road surface were the only signs of the other car. A short distance away, a couple of rotating wheels stuck up from the ditch.*

All of us began running towards it and then stopped in astonishment. The overturned car's radio sang a morning hymn. Two people crawled out of the ditch, a man and a woman, in the midst of a violent quarrel which was on the verge of coming to blows. When they saw us watching they immediately stopped and the man limped towards me.

ALMAN : How are you? There's nothing for me to say. The blame is completely ours. We have no excuses. It was my wife who was driving. Are you all right? Everyone safe and sound? Thank God for that.

He mumbled nervously, took off his glasses and put them on again, and looked at us with frightened glances.

ALMAN : The would-be murderers should introduce themselves. Alman is my name. I'm an engineer at the Stockholm electric power plant. Back there is my wife, Berit. She used to be an actress, and it was that fact we were discussing when . . . when . . . when . . .

He interrupted himself with an artificial laugh and waved at his wife. When she remained motionless, he took a few limping steps towards her.

ISAK : How is your leg?

ALMAN : It's not from this. I've been crippled for years. Unfortunately it's not only my leg that's crippled, according to my wife. Come here now, Berit, and make your apologies.

The woman mustered her courage. She moved jerkily in spite of her rotund body.

BERIT : Please, pretty please forgive me, as children say. It was my fault, everything. I was just going to hit my husband when that curve appeared. One thing is obvious: God punishes some people immediately — or what do you think, Sten? You're a Catholic.

ISAK : Perhaps we should take a look at your car and see if we can't put it right side up again.

ALMAN : Please don't trouble yourself over us. I beg of you.

BERIT : Shut up now, Sten darling. Some people do have completely unselfish intentions, even if you don't believe it.

ALMAN : My wife is a little nervous, I think. But we've had a shock. That's the word. A shock.

He laughed once more and tore off his glasses and put them on again. The young men had already jumped down into the ditch and were trying to lift the little car. MARIANNE ran back to our car and backed it down the road. With the help of a rope which I always carry in the boot, we succeeded in getting the other car on an even keel. MR ALMAN suddenly cheered up, threw off his jacket and rolled up his shirt sleeves. Then he put his shoulder alongside SARA, VIKTOR and ANDERS and began to push. (Still on page 40)

BERIT : Now watch the engineer closely, see how he matches his strength with the young boys, how he tenses his feeble muscles to impress the pretty girl. Sten darling, watch out that you don't have a haemorrhage.

ALMAN : My wife loves to embarrass me in front of strangers.

I let her — it's psychotherapy.

We towed and shoved and pushed and suddenly the little car was standing on the road. (Stills on page 40 and 57) By then, of course, its radio had gone dead. ALMAN sat down behind the wheel of the dented car and got the motor started. The car had gone a few feet when one of the front wheels rolled off abruptly and slid far down into the ravine.

BERIT : A true picture of our marriage.

ALMAN stood hesitantly on the gleaming white road, perspiring nervously. MARIANNE, who had stayed out of the whole scene, was still sitting behind the wheel of our car. The youngsters sat down at the edge of the road. All of us were a little upset.

ISAK : I can't see any other way out. The lady and the gentleman must ride with us to the nearest petrol station. There you can telephone for help.

ALMAN : Don't trouble yourself over us. We'll have a refreshing walk. Won't we, Berit?

BERIT : With his leg. Dear Lord, that would be a scream.

ALMAN : In her delightful way my wife has just said thank you for both of us.

Silently we climbed into the car, which was suddenly completely filled. (MARIANNE drove; I sat beside her. MR. and MRS. ALMAN were on the folding seats. The three youngsters occupied the back seat.) ALMAN whistled some popular tune softly but soon fell silent. No one had any particular desire to converse. MARIANNE drove very calmly and carefully.

Suddenly BERIT ALMAN started to cry. Her husband carefully put his arm around her shoulders, but she drew away and pulled out a handkerchief, which she began tearing with her fingernails.

ALMAN : I can never tell if my wife is really crying or putting on an act. Dammit, I think these are real tears. Well, that's the way it is when you see death staring you in the face.

BERIT : Can't you shut up?

ALMAN : My wife has unusual powers of the imagination. For two years she made me believe that she had cancer and pestered all our friends with all kinds of imaginary symptoms, despite the fact that the doctors couldn't find anything the matter. She was so convincing that we believed her more than the doctors. That's pretty clever, admit it. It's such stuff that saints are made of! Look, now she's crying about a death scare. It's a pity we don't have a movie camera around. Lights! Action! Camera! It's a 'take', as they say in the film world.

MARIANNE : It's understandable that you're upset, Mr. Alman, but how about leaving your wife alone for a little while?

ALMAN : A woman's tears are meant for women. Don't criticize a woman's tears — they're holy. You are beautiful, dear Miss whatever your name is. But Berit here is beginning to get a little shabby. That's why you can afford to defend her.

MARIANNE : Allow me to feel compassion for your wife for different reasons.

ALMAN : Very sarcastic! Still, you don't seem to be at all hysterical. But Berit is a genius at hysterics. Do you know what that means from my point of view? *(Still on page 57)*

MARIANNE : You're a Catholic, aren't you? That's what your wife said.

ALMAN : Quite right. That is my way of enduring. I ridicule my wife and she ridicules me. She has her hysterics and I have my Catholicism. But we need each other's company. It's only out of pure selfishness that we haven't murdered each other by now.*

> BERIT *turned towards her husband and slapped his face. He dropped his glasses, which he had fortunately just taken off. His large nose swelled and began to bleed. His froglike mouth twitched spasmodically as if he were on the verge of tears, but he immediately got control of himself, pulled out a handkerchief and pressed it to his nose, blinked his eyes and laughed.* VIKTOR *leaned forward, picked up the glasses and slowly handed them to him.*

ALMAN : Right on the beat. It's called syncopation, isn't it?

---

* In the film, after Alman's speech, we see Isak looking out of the window of the car. *(Still on page 58)*

Ha-ha! Isn't it comic? If I had a stop watch, I could have timed the explosion on the nose.

BERIT *screams* : Shut up! Shut up! Shut up!

> MARIANNE *turned pale. She applied the brakes and slowly stopped the car.*

MARIANNE : Maybe this is the terrible truth and maybe it's just what's called letting off steam. But we have three children in the car and for their sake may I ask the lady and the gentleman to get out immediately. There is a house back there; maybe they have a telephone. The walk won't be too strenuous.

> *All of us were silent after* MARIANNE's *speech. Without another word,* STEN ALMAN *stepped out of the car. His face was ashen grey and his nose was still bleeding. His wife looked at us and suddenly made a heroic attempt to say something sincere.*

BERIT : Forgive us if you can.

> *Then* BERIT *got out and stood by her husband, who had turned his back on us. He had pulled out a comb and a pocket mirror and was straightening the hair on his white scalp. His wife took his bloody handkerchief and blew her nose. Then she touched his elbow, but he was suddenly very tired and hung his head. They sat down close to each other by the road. They looked like two scolded schoolchildren sitting in a corner.*

> MARIANNE *started the car, and we quickly drove away from this strange marriage.*

> *The petrol station between Gränna and Huskvarna lies on a hill with a wide view over a very beautiful, richly foliaged landscape. We stopped to fill up the tank and decided to have lunch at a hotel some kilometers farther south.*

> *It was with mixed feelings that I saw this region again. First, because I began my medical practice here (incidentally, it lasted for fifteen years; I succeeded the local doctor). Second, because my old mother lives near here in a large house. She is ninety-six now and is generally considered a miracle of health and vitality, although her*

*ability to move around has diminished considerably
during the last few years.*

*The petrol-station owner was a big, blond man with a
broad face, abnormally large hands and long arms.*

AKERMAN : Ah ha ! So the doctor is out driving. Shall it be a
full tank ? Well, well, so it is, and those are children and
grandchildren, I know. Have you got the key to the petrol
tank, Doctor ?

ISAK : Hello, Henrik. You recognise me.

AKERMAN : Recognise ! Doctor, you were there when I was
born. And then you delivered all my brothers. And fixed
our cuts and scratches and took care of us, as you did of
everybody while you were a doctor around here.

ISAK : And things are going well for you ?

AKERMAN : Couldn't be better ! I'm married, you know, and
I have heirs. *Shouts* Eva !

> EVA *came out of the petrol-station. She was a young
> woman, gypsy-like, with long, thick hair and a generous
> smile. She was in an advanced stage of pregnancy.*

AKERMAN : Here you see Dr. Borg himself in person. This
is the man that Ma and Pa and the whole district still talk
about. The world's best doctor.

> *I looked at* MARIANNE *who was standing to the side. She
> applauded somewhat sarcastically and bowed. The three
> youngsters were in the midst of a lively dispute and
> pointing in different directions.* EVA *stepped up and
> shook my hand.*

AKERMAN : I suggest that we name our new baby for the
doctor. Isak Akerman is a good name for a prime minister.

EVA : But what if it's a girl ?

AKERMAN : Eva and I only make boys. Do you want oil and
water too ?

ISAK : Yes, thank you. And your father is well, in spite of his
bad back ?

AKERMAN : Well, it's getting a bit hard for the old man, you
know, but the old lady is a little bombshell.

> *The last was said in greatest confidence as we bent over
> the dip stick to see if we needed more oil. We did.*

AKERMAN : And now you'll be visiting *your* mother, eh,

Doctor?

ISAK : I suppose so.

AKERMAN : She's a remarkable lady, your mother, although she must be at least ninety-five.

ISAK : Ninety-six.

AKERMAN : Well, well, how about that.

ISAK : How much is all this?

AKERMAN : Eva and I want it to be on the house.

ISAK : No, I can't allow that.

AKERMAN : Don't insult us, Doctor! We can do things in the grand manner, too, even if we live here in little Gränna.

ISAK : There isn't the slightest reason you should pay for my petrol. I appreciate your kindness, but . . .

AKERMAN : One remembers things, you know. One doesn't forget one's gratitude, and there are some things that can never be paid back.

AKERMAN became a little serious and I a little sentimental. We looked at each other quite moved. EVA stepped up and stood beside her husband. She squinted in the sun and beamed like a big strawberry in her red dress.

EVA *like an echo* : No, we don't forget. We don't forget.

AKERMAN : Just ask anybody in town or in the hills around here, and they remember the doctor and know what the doctor did for them.

I looked around, but MARIANNE had disappeared. No, she had got into the car. The youngsters were still busy with their discussion.

ISAK : Perhaps I should have remained here.

AKERMAN : I don't understand.

ISAK : What? What did you say, Henrik?

AKERMAN : You said that you should have stayed here, Doctor.

ISAK : Did I say that? Yes, perhaps. Thank you anyway. Send me word and I may come to be godfather for the new Akerman. You know where to reach me.

I shook hands with them and we parted. MARIANNE called the youngsters and we continued our trip to the inn.

Our lunch was a success. We had a large table on the open terrace and enjoyed a most magnificent view across Lake Vättern. (Still on page 58) The head waiter, one of my former patients, did everything to satisfy our slightest wish.

I became very lively, I must admit, and told the youngsters about my years as a country doctor. I told them humorous anecdotes which had a great deal of human interest. These were a great success (I don't think they laughed just out of politeness) and I had wine with the food (which was excellent) and cognac with my coffee.

ANDERS *suddenly rose and began to recite with both feeling and talent.*

ANDERS : 'Oh, when such beauty shows itself in each facet of creation, then how beautiful must be the eternal source of this emanation!'

None of us thought of laughing at him. He sat down immediately and emptied his coffee cup in embarrassment. SARA *was the one who broke the silence.*

SARA : Anders will become a minister and Viktor a doctor.

VIKTOR : We swore that we wouldn't discuss God or science on the entire trip. I consider Anders' lyrical outburst as a breach of our agreement.

SARA : Oh, it was beautiful!

VIKTOR : Besides, I can't understand how a modern man can become a minister. Anders isn't a complete idiot.

ANDERS : Let me tell you, your rationalism is incomprehensible nonsense. And you aren't an idiot either.

VIKTOR : In my opinion the modern —

ANDERS : In my opinion —

VIKTOR : In my opinion a modern man looks his insignificance straight in the eye and believes in himself and his biological death. Everything else is nonsense.

ANDERS : And in my opinion modern man exists only in your imagination. Because man looks at his death with horror and can't bear his own insignificance.

VIKTOR : All right. Religion for the people. Opium for the aching limb. If that's what you want.

SARA : Aren't they fantastically sweet? I always agree with the one who's spoken last. Isn't this all extremely interesting?

VIKTOR *angry* : When you were a child you believed in Santa

56

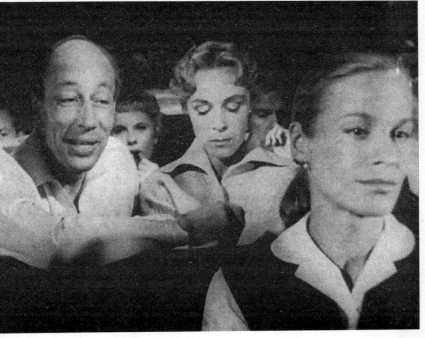

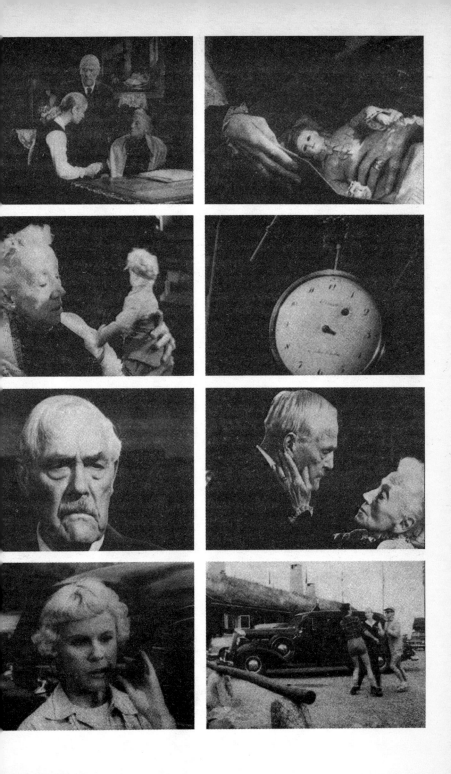

Claus. Now you believe in God.

ANDERS : And you have always suffered from an astonishing lack of imagination.

VIKTOR : What do you think about it, Professor?

ISAK : Dear boys, you would receive my opinion with ironic indulgence, whatever I happened to say. That's why I'm keeping quiet.

SARA : Then think how very unlucky they are.

ISAK : No, Sara. They are very, very lucky.

> MARIANNE *laughed and lit my cigar. I leaned back in my chair and squinted at the light filtering down between the table umbrellas. The boys looked surprised as I began to recite.*

ISAK : ' Where is the friend I seek everywhere? Dawn is the time of loneliness and care. When twilight comes, when twilight comes . . .' What comes after that, Anders?

MARIANNE : ' When twilight comes I am still yearning.'

ANDERS : ' Though my heart is burning, burning. I see His trace of glory . . .'

SARA : You're religious, aren't you, Professor?

ISAK : ' I see His trace of glory and power, In an ear of grain and the fragrance of flower . . .'

MARIANNE : ' In every sign and breath of air. His love is there. His voice whispers in the summer breeze . . .'

> *Silence.*

VIKTOR : As a love poem, it isn't too bad.

SARA : Now I've become very solemn. I can become quite solemn for no reason at all.

> *I rose from the table.*

ISAK : I want to pay a visit to my mother, who happens to live nearby. You can remain here and enjoy yourselves for a while. I'll be back soon.

MARIANNE : May I come with you?

ISAK : Of course. Goodbye for now, young friends.

> *I was in a good mood and felt very happy.* MARIANNE *suddenly took my arm and walked beside me. In passing, I patted her hand.*
>
> *The house was surrounded by an ancient, parklike garden and protected from onlookers by a wall as tall*

*as a man. Inside, everything was quiet and somewhat
unreal. The sky had clouded over, and the grey light
sharpened the contours of the landscape so that it looked
like a skillfully painted set in an old theatre.*

*In a little round drawing-room filled with storm-grey
light and graced by light, delicate furniture, an old nurse
in uniform sat embroidering. On the carpet next to her
chair a fat white poodle lay looking at us with sleepy,
lidded eyes. When the nurse saw us she immediately arose,
smiling politely, to greet us and shake our hands. She
introduced herself as Sister* ELISABET. *I asked her quietly
how my mother was and if it was convenient for us to
visit her. Sister* ELISABET *answered that* MRS. BORG *was
quite well and would be happy with our visit because
she was usually rather lonely. I pointed out that it was
unfortunate that my visits were rather infrequent, because
of the difficult journey, and Sister* ELISABET *said that
she understood. After this hushed introduction, the Sister
asked us to wait for a few minutes and disappeared into a
nearby room.* MARIANNE *became a little nervous with all
the solemnity and pulled out a cigarette from a crushed
pack and was just about to light it.*

ISAK : Please don't smoke. Mother hates the smell of tobacco
and her senses are as sharp as those of an animal in the woods.

At the same moment, Sister ELISABET *returned and told
us that we were welcome.*

*The room was rather small and oddly irregular, but it
had a lofty ceiling. On the walls hung many beautiful
and expensive paintings. Heavy draperies covered the
doors. In a corner stood a tall porcelain stove with a
fire burning. At the room's only window stood an
incongruous desk which did not harmonize with the
other pieces of furniture. My mother was sitting in a big
chair. She was dressed entirely in black and wore a
small lace cap on her head. She was busy entering figures
in a large blue ledger. When she recognised me, she
immediately rose from her seat (although with some
difficulty) and walked towards us with many small steps;
she seemed to be shoving one foot in front of the other*

without her soles ever leaving the floor. She smiled cordially and stretched forth both her hands. I grasped them and then kissed her with a son's reverence.

MOTHER : I just sent a telegram to tell you that I was thinking about you today. Today is your big day. And then you come here!

ISAK : Well, I had a moment of inspiration, Mother!

MOTHER : Is that your wife standing back there, Isak? You will ask her to leave the room immediately. I refuse to talk with her. She has hurt us too much.

ISAK : Mother, darling, this is not Karin. This is Evald's wife, my daughter-in-law, Marianne!

MOTHER : Well, then, she can come here and greet me.

MARIANNE : How do you do, Mrs. Borg. *Curtsies. (Still on page 59)*

MOTHER : I've seen you in a photograph. Evald showed it to me. He was extremely proud of your beauty. By the way, why are you travelling this way?

MARIANNE : I've been in Stockholm, visiting.

MOTHER : Why aren't you home with Evald and taking care of your child?

MARIANNE : Evald and I don't have any children.

MOTHER : Isn't it strange with young people nowadays? I bore ten children. Will someone please bring me that large box standing over there.

She pointed at a brown cardboard box on a chair. MARIANNE picked it up and placed it on the desk in front of the old lady. Both of us helped lift the lid.

MOTHER : My mother lived in this house before me. And you children often visited here. Do you remember, Isak?

ISAK : I remember quite well.

MOTHER : In this box are some of your toys. I've tried to think which of you owned what.

MOTHER looked bewilderedly into the big box, as if she expected to find all her children there among the toys and things. Then she shook her head and looked up at MARIANNE.

MOTHER : Ten children, and all of them dead except Isak. Twenty grandchildren. None of them visits me except Evald,

63

once a year. It's quite all right — I don't complain — but I have fifteen great-grandchildren whom I've never seen. I send letters and presents for fifty-three birthdays and anniversaries every year. I get kind thank-you notes, but no one visits me except by accident or when someone needs a loan. I am tiresome, of course.

ISAK : Don't look at it that way, Mother dear!

MOTHER : And then I have another fault. I don't die. The inheritance doesn't materialise according to the nice, neat schedules made up by smart young people.

She laughed sarcastically and shook her head. Then she pulled a doll out of the box. It was an old doll, with fine gold hair and a porcelain face (a little scratched) and a beautiful lace gown. (Still on page 59)

MOTHER : This doll's name is Goldcrown and it belonged to Sigbritt. She got it when she was eight years old. I sewed the dress myself. She never liked it much, so Charlotta took it over and cared for it. I remember it clearly. *(Still on page 59)*

She dropped the doll and picked up a little box of bright-coloured tin soldiers and poked in it with a small, sharp finger.

MOTHER : Hagbart's tin soldiers. I never liked his war games. He was shot while hunting moose. We never understood each other.

This she said in a matter-of-fact tone, completely without sentimentality. She threw the tin soldiers into the box and fished out a photograph.

MOTHER : Can you see who this is? This is Sigfrid when he was three years old and you when you were two, and here is Father and me. Good Lord, how one looked in those days. It was taken in 1883.

ISAK : May I see that picture?

MOTHER *uninterested* : Yes, of course, you can have it. It's only trash. Here is a colouring book. Maybe it belonged to the twins, or perhaps to Anna or Angelica. I really don't know because all of them have put their names in the book. And then it says : ' I am Anna's best friend.' But Anna has written : ' I love Angelica.' and Kristina has scribbled : ' Most of all in the whole world I love Father best.' And Birgitta has added:

' I am going to marry Father.' Isn't that amusing? I laughed when I read it.

MARIANNE *took the book from her and turned the pages. It was partly scribbled on and partly painted with great vitality and strong colours. The light in the small room grew dimmer as the sky darkened outside. In the distance the thunder was already rumbling in the sky.* MOTHER *picked up a toy locomotive and looked at it closely.*

MOTHER : I think that this is Benjamin's locomotive because he was always so amused by trains and circuses and such things. I suppose that's why he became an actor. We quarrelled often about it because I wanted him to have an honest profession. And I was right. He didn't make it. I told him that several times. He didn't believe me, but I was right. It doesn't pay much to talk. Isn't it cold in here? The fire doesn't really warm.

ISAK : No, it isn't particularly cold.

She turned her head towards the darkened skies outside. The trees stood heavy, as if waiting.

MOTHER : I've always felt chilly as long as I can remember. What does that mean? You're a doctor? Mostly in the stomach. Here.

ISAK : You have low blood pressure.

MOTHER : Do you want me to ask Sister Elisabet to make some tea for us so we can sit down and talk for a while? Wouldn't that be . . .

ISAK : No, Mother, thank you. We don't want to trouble you any more. We've just had lunch and we're rather in a hurry.

MOTHER : Look here for a moment. Sigbritt's eldest boy will be fifty. I'm thinking of giving him my father's old gold watch. Can I give it to him, even though the hands have loosened? It is so difficult to find presents for those who have everything. But the watch is beautiful and it can probably be repaired.

She looked anxiously, appealingly, from MARIANNE *to me and back to* MARIANNE. *She had opened the lid of the old gold watch and the blank dial stared at me. (Still on page 59) I suddenly remembered my early-morning dream: the blank clock face and my own watch which*

lacked hands, the hearse and my dead self. (Still on
page 59)

MOTHER : I remember when Sigbritt's boy had just been born and lay there in his basket in the lilac arbour at the summer-house. Now he will be fifty years old. And little cousin Sara, who always went around carrying him, cradling him, and who married Sigfrid, that no-good. Now you have to go so that you'll have time for all the things you must do. I'm very grateful for your visit and I hope we'll see each other some time. Give my best regards to Evald. Goodbye. *(Still on page*
59)

> *She offered me her cheek and I bent down and kissed it.*
> *It was very cold but unbelievably soft and full of sharp*
> *little lines.* MARIANNE *curtsied and my mother answered*
> *her gesture with an abstract smile. Sister* ELISABET *opened*
> *the door as if she had been listening to us. In a few*
> *minutes we were out in the grey daylight, which hurt*
> *our eyes with its piercing sharpness.*
> *Once again* MARIANNE *took my arm, and when she did*
> *so I was filled with gratitude towards this quiet, indepen-*
> *dent girl with her naked, observant face.*
> *When we reached the inn the youngsters were no*
> *longer there. The waitress told us that the young lady*
> *was waiting at the car. The head waiter stood nearby*
> *bowing and looking as if he had just had another of his*
> *old ulcer-attacks.*
> *Sure enough,* SARA *was leaning against the car looking*
> *as though she were ready to cry. (Still on page 59)*

MARIANNE : Where are Anders and Viktor ?

> SARA *pointed without answering. Down on the slope the*
> *boys stood glaring at each other with furious expressions*
> *on their faces. Every so often one of them would utter*
> *some terrible expletive at the other.*

SARA : When you left they were talking away about the existence of God. Finally they got so angry that they began shouting at each other. Then Anders grabbed Viktor's arm and tried to twist it off, and Viktor said that was a pretty lousy argument for the existence of God. Then I said that I thought they could skip God and pay some attention to me for a

66

while instead, and then they said that I could stop babbling because I didn't understand that it was a debate of principles, and then I said that whether there was a God or not, they were real wet blankets. Then I left and they ran down the hill to settle things because each of them insisted that the other had hurt his innermost feelings. So now they're going to slug it out.

MARIANNE *put on a very wise countenance and started off to calm down the two debaters. I stepped into the car.*

SARA *looked at the departing* MARIANNE *with envy.*

SARA : Well, which one of the boys do *you* like the most?

ISAK : Which do you like best?

SARA : I don't know. Anders will become a minister. But he is rather masculine and warm, you know. But a minister's wife! But Viktor's funny in another way. Viktor will go far, you know.

ISAK : What do you mean by that?

SARA *tired* : A doctor earns more money. And it's old-fashioned to be a minister. But he has nice legs. And a strong neck. But how *can* one believe in God!

SARA *sighed and we sank into our own thoughts.*

MARIANNE *came up the hill bringing with her the two fighting cocks, barely reconciled. (Still on page 59) She sat down behind the wheel and we continued our trip.*

The sun shone white on the blue-black clouds which towered above the dark, gleaming surface of Lake Vättern. The breeze coming from the open side windows did not cool us any longer, and in the south summer lightning cut across the sky with thin, jagged scratches. Because of the approaching storm, and all the good food and wine, I became rather sleepy. I silently blessed my luck in having MARIANNE *beside me as a reliable chauffeur.*

ANDERS *and* VIKTOR *sat in sullen silence.* SARA *yawned again and again and blinked her eyes.*

I fell asleep, but during my nap I was pursued by dreams and images which seemed extremely real and were very humiliating to me.

I record these in the order in which they occurred,

without the slightest intention of commenting on their possible meaning. I have never been particularly enthusiastic about the psychoanalytical theory of dreams as the fulfillment of desires in a negative or positive direction. Yet I cannot deny that in these dreams there was something like a warning, which bore into my consciousness and embedded itself there with relentless determination. I have found that during the last few years I glide rather easily into a twilight world of memories and dreams which are highly personal. I've often wondered if this is a sign of increasing senility. Sometimes I've also asked myself if it is a harbinger of approaching death.*

Again I found myself at the wild strawberry patch of my childhood, but I was not alone. SARA was there, and this time she turned her face towards mine and looked at me for a long time. I knew that I sat there looking old, ugly and ridiculous. A Professor Emeritus who was going to be made a Jubilee Doctor. The saddest thing about it was that although SARA spoke to me in a grieved and penetrating tone, I couldn't answer her except in stammered, one-syllable words. This, of course, increased the pain of my dream.

Between us stood a little woven basket filled with strawberries; around us lay a strange, motionless twilight, heavy with dull expectations. SARA leaned towards me and spoke in such a low voice that I had difficulty grasping her words.

SARA : Have you looked at yourself in the mirror, Isak? You haven't. Then I'll show you how you look.

She picked up a mirror that lay hidden under the small strawberry basket and showed me my face, which looked old and ugly in the sinking twilight. I carefully pushed away the looking glass and I could see that SARA had

---

* In the film, as the dream sequence begins the following shots are seen :

Dissolve to the dark sky with large birds circling, wheeling and shrieking. Dissolve to more large birds flying among the tree tops. (Still on page 60). Dissolve to a basket of wild strawberries spilled on the grass. (Still on page 60).

tears in her eyes.

SARA : You are a worried old man who will die soon, but I have my whole life before me . . . Oh, now you're offended. *(Still on page 60)*

ISAK : No, I'm not offended.

SARA : Yes, you are offended because you can't bear to hear the truth. And the truth is that I've been too considerate. One can easily be unintentionally cruel that way.

ISAK : I understand.

SARA : No, you don't understand. We don't speak the same language. Look at yourself in the mirror again. No, don't look away.

ISAK : I see.

SARA : Now listen. I'm about to marry your brother Sigfrid. He and I love each other, and it's all like a game. Look at your face now. Try to smile! All right, now you're smiling.

ISAK : It hurts.

SARA : You, a Professor Emeritus, ought to know why it hurts. But you don't. Because in spite of all your knowledge you don't really know anything.

> *She threw away the mirror and it shattered. The wind began to blow through the trees, and from somewhere the crying of a child could be heard. She arose immediately, drying her tears.*

SARA : I have to go. I promised to look after Sigbritt's little boy.

ISAK : Don't leave me.

SARA : What did you say?

ISAK : Don't leave me.

SARA : You stammer so much that I can't hear your words. Besides, they don't really matter.

> *I saw her run up to the arbour. (Still on page 60) The old house was draped in the grey twilight. She lifted the crying child and cradled it in her arms. (Still on page 60) The sky turned black above the sea and large birds circled overhead, screeching towards the house, which suddenly seemed ugly and poor. There was something fateful and threatening in this twilight, in the crying of the child, in the shrieking of the black birds. SARA cradled the baby*

and her voice, half singing, was very distant and sorrow-ful.

SARA : My poor little one, you shall sleep quietly now. Don't be afraid of the wind. Don't be afraid of the birds, the jack-daws and the sea gulls. Don't be afraid of the waves from the sea. I'm with you. I'm holding you tight. Don't be afraid, little one. Soon it will be another day. No one can hurt you; I am with you; I'm holding you.

But her voice was sorrowful and tears ran down her cheeks without end. The child became silent, as if it were listening, and I wanted to scream until my lungs were bloody.

Now I saw that a door had opened in the house and someone was standing there shouting for SARA. *It was my brother* SIGFRID.

She ran towards him, gave him the child, and they both disappeared into the house and closed the door.

Suddenly I noticed that the wind had died and the birds had flown away. All the windows in the house shone festively. Over the horizon stood a jagged moon, and music from a piano penetrated the stillness of the strawberry patch.

I went closer and pressed my face against the brightly lit dining-room window. An elegantly laid table stood before me and SARA *sat behind the piano, playing. She was wearing an expensive but old-fashioned dress and her hair was piled on top of her head, which made her face look womanly and mature. (Still on page 60) Then* SIGFRID *entered the room and they both sat down im-mediately at the table. They laughed and joked and celebrated some kind of event. The moon rose higher in the heavens and the scene inside became obscure. I rapped on the window so that they would hear me and let me in. But they did not notice me; they were too pre-occupied with each other.*

On the window sill lay many splinters of glass, and in my eager attempt to get their attention I accidently cut my hand.

Turning away, I was blinded by the moonlight, which

70

threw itself against me with an almost physical force.

I heard a voice calling my name, and then I saw that the door had been opened. Someone was standing in the doorway and I recognised MR. ALMAN. *He bowed politely though stiffly and invited me inside.*

He led me down a short corridor and unlocked a narrow door. We entered a large windowless room with benches arranged like an amphitheatre. There sat about ten youngsters, amongst whom I immediately recognised SARA, ANDERS *and* VIKTOR. *On one of the low walls hung a large blackboard, and on a work table in the centre of the room stood a microscope.*

I realised that this was the hall where I used to hold my polyclinical lectures and examinations. ALMAN *sat down and asked me to take a seat at the short end of the table. For a few moments he studied some papers in a dossier. The audience remained completely still. (Still on page 60)*

ALMAN : Do you have your examination book with you?

ISAK : Yes, of course. Here it is.

ALMAN : Thank you.

I handed him the examination book and he flipped through it distractedly. Then he leaned forward and looked at me for a long time. After that he gestured towards the microscope.

ALMAN : Will you please identify the bacteriological specimen in the microscope. Take your time.

I arose, stepped up to the instrument and adjusted it. But whatever I did, I couldn't find any specimen. The only thing I saw was my own eye, which stared back at me in an absurd enlargement.

ISAK : There must be something wrong with the microscope.

ALMAN *bent over and peered into it. Then he regarded me seriously and shook his head.*

ALMAN : There is nothing wrong with the microscope.

ISAK : I can't see anything. *(Still on page 60)*

I sank down on the chair and wetted my lips. No one moved or said anything.

ALMAN : Will you please read this text.

71

He pointed to the blackboard which hung behind him. Something was printed on it in large crooked letters. I made a great effort to interpret what was written: INKE TAN MAGROV STAK FARSIN LOS KRET FAJNE KASERTE MJOTRON PRESETE.

ALMAN : What does it mean?

ISAK : I don't know.

ALMAN : Oh, really?

ISAK : I'm a doctor, not a linguist.

ALMAN : Then let me tell you, Professor Borg, that on the blackboard is written the first duty of a doctor. Do you happen to know what this is?

ISAK : Yes, if you let me think for a moment.

ALMAN : Take your time.

ISAK : A doctor's first duty . . . a doctor's first duty . . . a doctor's . . . Oh, I've forgotten.

> *A cold sweat broke out on my forehead, but I still looked ALMAN straight in the eye. He leaned towards me and spoke in a calm, polite tone.*

ALMAN : A doctor's first duty *is to ask forgiveness. (Still on page 77)*

ISAK : Of course, now I remember!

> *Relieved, I laughed but immediately became silent. ALMAN looked wearily at his papers and smothered a yawn.*

ALMAN : Moreover, you are guilty of guilt.

ISAK : Guilty of guilt?

ALMAN : I have noted that you don't understand the accusation.

ISAK : Is it serious? *(Still on page 77)*

ALMAN : Unfortunately, Professor.

> *Next to me stood a table with a water decanter. I poured a glass, but spilled a lot of it on the table and the tray. (Still on page 77)*

ISAK : I have a bad heart. I'm an old man, Mr. Alman, and I must be treated with consideration. That's only right.

ALMAN : There is nothing concerning your heart in my papers. Perhaps you wish to end the examination?

ISAK : No, no, for heaven's sake, no!

ALMAN *arose and lit a small lamp which hung from a cord in the ceiling. Under the lamp (very brightly lit) sat a woman wrapped in a hospital robe and wearing wooden sandals on her feet. (Still on page 77)*

ALMAN : Will you please make an anamnesis and diagnosis of this patient.

ISAK : But the patient is dead.

At that moment the woman arose and began laughing as if she had just heard a great joke. ALMAN *leaned across the table and wrote something in my examination book.*

ISAK : What are you writing in my book?

ALMAN : My conclusion.

ISAK : And that is . . .

ALMAN : That you're incompetent.

ISAK : Incompetent.

ALMAN : Furthermore, Professor Borg, you are accused of some smaller but nonetheless serious offences. ISAK *remains silent.* Indifference, selfishness, lack of consideration.

ISAK : No.

ALMAN : These accusations have been made by your wife. Do you want to be confronted by her?

ISAK : But my wife has been dead for many years.

ALMAN : Do you think I'm joking? Will you please come with me voluntarily. You have no choice in any case. Come!

ALMAN *placed the examination book in his pocket, made a sign for me to follow him, opened the door and led me into a forest.*

The trunks of the trees stood close together. Twilight had almost passed. Dead trees were strewn on the ground and the earth was covered with decaying leaves. Our feet sank into this soft carpet with every step, and mud oozed up around them. From behind the foliage the moon shone steadily, like an inflamed eye, and it was as warm as inside a hothouse. ALMAN *turned around.*

ALMAN : Watch out, Professor Borg. You'll find many snakes here.

Suddenly I saw a small, gleaming body which twisted around and disappeared in one of ALMAN's *wet footsteps. I stepped swiftly aside but nearly trod on a large grey*

73

*creature which pulled away. Wherever I looked, snakes
seemed to well forth from the swampy, porous ground.
Finally we arrived at a clearing in the forest, but we
halted at the very edge. The moon shone in our eyes and
we hid among the shadows of the trees. The clearing
stretched out before us. It was overgrown with twisted
roots. At one end a black cliff fell away into a body of
water. On the sides, the trees stood lofty and lifeless, as
if burdened by each other's enormous shadows. Then a
giggling laugh was heard and I discovered a woman
standing near the hill. She was dressed in a long black
gown and her face was averted from us. She made move-
ments with her hands, as if to ward off someone. She
laughed continually and excitedly. A man stood half
hidden, leaning against a tree trunk. His face, which I
glimpsed, was large and flat, but his eyebrows were quite
bushy and his forehead protruded over his eyes. He made
gestures with his hand and said some unintelligible words,
which made the woman laugh uncontrollably. Suddenly
she became serious, and a harassed, discontented expression appeared on her face. She bent over and picked
up a small purse. The man stretched out his hand and
jokingly began to pull the pins out of her skilfully
pompadoured hair. She pretended to be very angry and
flailed the air around her furiously. This amused the man,
who continued his game. When she finally walked away
he followed and took hold of her shoulders. Petrified, she
stopped and turned her pale, embittered face towards her
pursuer. He muttered something and stretched out his
other hand towards her breast. She moved away, but
couldn't free herself. When she saw that she was caught,
she began to twist and squirm as if the man's grip on her
shoulders hurt intensely. The man continued to mutter
incoherent words, as if to an animal. Suddenly she freed
herself and ran with bent knees and a shuffling step in a
semicircle. The man remained standing, waiting and
breathless. He perspired heavily and wiped his face over
and over again with the back of his hand. The woman
stopped as if exhausted and regarded the man, wide-eyed*

74

*and gaping. She was also out of breath. Then she began
running again but pretended to trip and fell on her
hands and knees. Her large rump swayed like a black
balloon over the ground. She lowered her face between
her arms and began crying, rocking and swaying. The
man knelt at her side, took a firm grasp of her hair,
pulled her face upward, backward and forced her to
open her eyes. He panted with effort the whole time. She
teetered and nearly fell to the side, but the man straddled
her and leaned over her heavily. Suddenly she was completely still, with closed eyes and a swollen, pale face.
Then she collapsed, rolled over, and received the man
between her open knees. (Stills on page 77)*

ALMAN: Many men forget a woman who has been dead for
thirty years. Some preserve a sweet, fading picture, but *you*
can always recall this scene in your memory. Strange, isn't it?
Tuesday, May 1, 1917, you stood here and heard and saw
exactly what that woman and that man said and did. *(Still
on page 77)*

*The woman sat up and smoothed her gown over her
short, thick thighs. Her face was blank and almost
distorted in its puffy slackness. The man had got up and
was wandering around aimlessly with his hands hanging
at his sides.*

WOMAN: Now I will go home and tell this to Isak and I
know exactly what he'll say: Poor little girl, how I pity you.
As if he were God himself. And then I'll cry and say: Do you
really feel pity for me? And he'll say: I feel infinitely sorry
for you. And then I'll cry some more and ask him if he can
forgive me. And then he'll say: You shouldn't ask forgiveness
from me. I have nothing to forgive. But he doesn't mean a
word of it, because he's completely cold. And then he'll
suddenly be very tender and I'll yell at him that he's not really
sane and that such hypocritical nobility is sickening. And
then he'll say that he'll bring me a sedative and that he
understands everything. And then I'll say that it's his fault
that I am the way I am, and then he'll look very sad and
will say that he is to blame. But he doesn't care about anything because he's completely cold.

75

She arose with effort and shook out her hair and began combing it and pinning it up in the same careful way that it was before. The man sat down on a stone a little further away. He smoked quietly. I couldn't see his gaze below the protruding eyebrows, but his voice was calm and scornful.

MAN : You're insane, the way you're carrying on.
The woman laughed and went into the forest.

I turned around. ALMAN *had a strange, wry smile on his face. We stood quietly for a few moments.*

ISAK : Where is she?

ALMAN : You know. She is gone. Everyone is gone. Can't you hear how quiet it is? Everything has been dissected, Professor Borg. A surgical masterpiece. There is no pain, no bleeding, no quivering.

ISAK : It is rather quiet.

ALMAN : A perfect achievement of its kind, Professor.

ISAK : And what is the penalty?

ALMAN : Penalty? I don't know. The usual one, I suppose.

ISAK : The usual one?

ALMAN : Of course. Loneliness.

ISAK : Loneliness?

ALMAN : Exactly. *Loneliness.*

ISAK : Is there no grace?

ALMAN : Don't ask me. I don't know anything about such things.
Before I had time to answer, ALMAN *had disappeared, and I stood alone in the complete stillness of the moonlight and the forest.* [*Then I heard a voice quite close to me.*

SARA : Didn't you have to go with them to get your father?
The girl stretched out her hand, but when she saw my face she immediately withdrew it.

ISAK : Sara . . . It wasn't always like this. If only you had stayed with me. If only you could have had a little patience.
The girl did not seem to hear what I was saying but began to look restless.

SARA : Hurry up.

76

I followed her as well as I could, but she moved so much more easily and faster than I.

ISAK : I can't run, don't you understand?

SARA : But hurry up.

ISAK : I can't see you any more.

SARA : But here I am.

ISAK : Wait for me.

She materialised for a moment and then she was gone. The moon disappeared into darkness and I wanted to cry with wild, childish sorrow, but I could not.]*

At that moment, I awoke. The car stood still and the storm was over, but it was still drizzling slightly. We were in the neighbourhood of the Strömsnäs Foundry, where the road wanders between rich forests on one side and river rapids on the other. Everything was completely silent. The three children had left the car and MARIANNE sat quietly smoking a cigarette and blowing the smoke through the open window. Gusts of strong and pleasant odours came from the wet forest.

ISAK : What is this?

MARIANNE : The children wanted to get out for a moment and stretch their legs. They are over there.

She made a gesture towards a clearing near the river. All three were busy picking flowers.

ISAK : But it's still raining.

MARIANNE : I told them about the ceremony today, and they insisted on paying homage to you.

ISAK *sighs* : Good Lord.

MARIANNE : Did you sleep well?

ISAK : Yes, but I dreamed. Can you imagine — the last few months I've had the most peculiar dreams. It's really odd.

MARIANNE : What's odd?

ISAK : It's as if I'm trying to say something to myself which I don't want to hear when I'm awake.

---

* The scene in square brackets does not appear in the print of the film distributed in England.

MARIANNE : And what would that be?

ISAK : That I'm dead, although I live.

> MARIANNE *reacted violently. Her gaze blackened and she took a deep breath. Throwing her cigarette out the window, she turned towards me.*

MARIANNE : Do you know that you and Evald are very much alike?

ISAK : You told me that.

MARIANNE : Do you know that Evald has said the very same thing?

ISAK : About me? Yes, I can believe that.

MARIANNE : No, about himself.

ISAK : But he's only thirty-eight years old.

MARIANNE : May I tell you everything, or would it bore you?

ISAK : I'd be grateful if you would tell me.

MARIANNE : It was a few months ago. I wanted to talk to Evald and we took the car and went down to the sea. It was raining, just like now. Evald sat where you are sitting and I drove. . . .

EVALD : Can't you stop the windshield wipers?

MARIANNE : Then we won't be able to see the ocean.

EVALD : They're working so hard it makes me nervous.

MARIANNE *shuts them off* : Very well.

> *They sit in silence for a few minutes, looking at the rain, which streams down the windshield quietly. The sea merges with the clouds in an infinite greyness.* EVALD *strokes his long, bony face and looks expectantly at his wife. He talks jokingly, calmly.*

EVALD : So now you have me trapped. What did you want to say? Something unpleasant, of course. *(Still on page 78)*

MARIANNE : I wish I didn't have to tell you about it.

EVALD : I understand. You've found someone else.

MARIANNE : Now don't be childish.

EVALD *mimicking her* : Now don't be childish. What do you expect me to think? You come and say in a funereal voice that you want to talk to me. We take the car and go down to the sea. It rains and it's hard for you to begin. Good Lord, Marianne, let's have it. This is an excellent moment for the most intimate confidence. But for heaven's sake, don't keep me dangling.

MARIANNE : Now I feel like laughing. What do you really think I'm going to say? That I've murdered someone, or embezzled the faculty funds? I'm pregnant, Evald.

EVALD : Oh, is that so.

MARIANNE : That's the way it is. And seeing how careless we've been recently, there isn't much to be surprised about, is there?

EVALD : And you're sure?

MARIANNE : The report on the test came yesterday.

EVALD : Oh. Oh, yes. So that was the secret.

MARIANNE : Another thing I want to tell you. I shall have this child.

EVALD : That seems to be clear.

MARIANNE : Yes, it is!

MARIANNE *voice over* : We sat quietly for a long time, and I felt the hatred growing big and thick between us. Evald looked out through the wet window, whistled soundlessly and looked as if he were cold. Somewhere in my stomach I was shivering so hard that I could barely sit upright. Then he opened the door and got out of the car and marched through the rain down to the beach. He stopped under a big tree and stood there for a long while. Finally I also stepped out and went to him. His face and hair were wet and the rain fell down his cheeks to the sides of his mouth.

EVALD *calmly* : You know that I don't want to have any children. You also know that you'll have to choose between me and the child.

MARIANNE *looks at him* : Poor Evald.

EVALD : Please don't ' poor ' me. I'm of sound mind and I've made my position absolutely clear. It's absurd to live in this world, but it's even more ridiculous to populate it with new victims and it's most absurd of all to believe that they will have it any better than us.

MARIANNE : That is only an excuse.

EVALD : Call it whatever you want. Personally I was an unwelcome child in a marriage which was a nice imitation of hell. Is the old man really sure that I'm his son? Indifference, fear, infidelity and guilt feelings — those were my nurses.

83

MARIANNE : All this is very touching, but it doesn't excuse the fact that you're behaving like a child.

EVALD : I have to be at the hospital at three o'clock and have neither the time nor the desire to talk any more.

MARIANNE : You're a coward!

EVALD : Yes, that's right. This life disgusts me and I don't think that I need a responsibility which will force me to exist another day longer than I want to. You know all that, and you know that I'm serious and that this isn't some kind of hysteria, as you once thought.

MARIANNE, *voice over* : We went towards the car, he in front and I following. I had begun to cry. I don't know why. But the tears couldn't be seen in the rain. We sat in the car, thoroughly wet and cold, but the hatred throbbed in us so painfully that we didn't feel cold. I started the car and turned it towards the road. Evald sat fiddling with the radio. His face was completely calm and closed.

MARIANNE : I know that you're wrong.

EVALD : There is nothing which can be called right or wrong. One functions according to one's needs; you can read that in an elementary-school textbook.

MARIANNE : And what do we need?

EVALD : You have a damned need to live, to exist and create life.

MARIANNE : And how about you?

EVALD : My need is to be dead. Absolutely, totally dead.

I've tried to relate MARIANNE's *story as carefully as possible. My reaction to it was very mixed. But my strongest feeling was a certain sympathy towards her for this sudden confidence, and when* MARIANNE *fell silent she looked so hesitant that I felt obliged to say something even though I wasn't very sure of my own voice.*

ISAK : If you want to smoke a cigarette, you may.

MARIANNE : Thank you.

ISAK : Why have you told me all this?

MARIANNE *didn't answer at once. She took her time lighting a cigarette and puffed a few times. I looked at her, but she turned her head away and pretended to look at the three youngsters, who had picked up some kind*

84

of soft drink which they shared in great amity.

MARIANNE : When I saw you together with your mother, I was gripped by a strange fear.

ISAK : I don't understand.

MARIANNE : I thought, here is his mother. A very ancient woman, completely ice-cold, in some ways more frightening than death itself. And here is her son, and there are light-years of distance between them. And he himself says that he is a living death. And Evald is on the verge of becoming just as lonely and cold — and dead. And then I thought that there is only coldness and death, and death and loneliness, all the way. Somewhere it must end.

ISAK : But you are going back to Evald.

MARIANNE : Yes, to tell him that I can't agree to his condition. I want my child; no one can take it from me. Not even the person I love more than anyone else.

> *She turned her pale, tearless face towards me, and her gaze was black, accusing, desperate. I suddenly felt shaken in a way which I had never experienced before.*

ISAK : Can I help you?

MARIANNE : No one can help me. We are too old, Isak. It has gone too far.

ISAK : What happened after your talk in the car?

MARIANNE : Nothing. I left him the very next day.

ISAK : Haven't you heard from him?

MARIANNE : No. No, Evald is rather like you.

> *She shook her head and bent forward as if to protect her face. I felt cold; it had become quite chilly after the rain.*

MARIANNE : Those two wretched people whom I made leave the car — what was their name again?

ISAK : I was just thinking about Alman and his wife. It reminded me of my own marriage.

MARIANNE : I don't want Evald and I to become like . . . (Still on page 78)

ISAK : Poor Evald grew up in all that.

MARIANNE : But we love each other.

> *Her last words were a low outburst. She stopped herself immediately and moved her hands towards her face,*

then stopped again. We sat quietly for a few moments.
ISAK : We must get on. Signal to the children.

> MARIANNE *nodded, started the motor and blew the horn.*
> SARA *came laughing through the wet grass, closely*
> *followed by her two cavaliers. She handed me a large*
> *bouquet of wild flowers wrapped in wet newspapers. All*
> *three of them had friendly, mocking eyes.* SARA *cleared*
> *her throat solemnly. (Still on page 79)*

SARA : We heard that you are celebrating this day. Now we
want to pay our respects to you with these simple flowers and
to tell you that we are *very* impressed that you are so old and
that you've been a doctor for fifty years. And we know, of
course, that you are a *wise* and *venerable* old man. One who
regards us youngsters with *lenience* and gentle irony. One who
knows *all* about life and who has learned all the prescriptions
by heart.

> *She gave me the flowers with a little mock curtsy and*
> *kissed my cheek. The boys bowed and laughed, em-*
> *barrassed. I couldn't answer. I only thanked them very*
> *briefly and rather bluntly. The children probably thought*
> *that I had been hurt by their joke.*

> *After a few more hours' travel, we reached Lund.*
> *When we finally stopped at* EVALD'S *house, a small*
> *rotund woman ran out and approached us quickly. To*
> *my surprise and pleasure I discovered that it was Miss*
> AGDA.

AGDA : So you did come. Evald and I had just given up
hope. It's relaxing and convenient to drive, isn't it? Now,
Professor, you'll have to put on your frock coat immediately.
Hello, Marianne. I've prepared Evald for your arrival.
ISAK : So, Miss Agda, you came after all.
AGDA : I considered it my duty. But the fun is gone. There's
nothing you can say that will make me feel different. Who are
these young people? Are they going to the ceremony too?
MARIANNE : These are good friends of ours, and if there is
any food in the kitchen, invite them in.
AGDA : And why shouldn't there be? I've had a lot of things
to arrange here, believe me.

EVALD *met us in the foyer. He was already dressed in evening clothes and seemed nervous. Everything was extremely confused, but Miss* AGDA *was a pillar of strength in the maelstrom. Without raising her voice, and dressed in her best dress (especially made for the occasion), she sent the children, the married couple, servants and an old professor in different directions. Within ten minutes, everything was in order.*

Just before that, EVALD, MARIANNE *and I had a chance to say hello. I wouldn't want to give the impression that our reunion was marked by overwhelming cordiality. This has never been the case in our family.*

EVALD : Hello, Father. Welcome.

ISAK : Hello, Evald, Thank you. As you can see, I brought Marianne with me.

EVALD : Hello, Marianne.

MARIANNE : Can I take my things upstairs?

EVALD : Do you want to stay in the guest room as usual, Father?

ISAK : Thank you, that would be just fine.

EVALD : Let me take your suitcase. It's rather heavy. *(Still on page 79)*

ISAK : Thank you, I'll take it myself.

EVALD : Did you have a nice trip?

MARIANNE : Yes, thanks it's been pleasant.

EVALD : Who were those youngsters you had with you?

MARIANNE : Don't know. They're going to Italy.

EVALD : They looked rather nice.

ISAK : They are really very nice.

We had come to the second floor. EVALD *politely opened the door to the guest room and I entered.* AGDA *came after us as if she were rolling on ball bearings, forced her way in and took the suitcase, putting it on a chair.*

AGDA : I bought new shoelaces, and I took the liberty of bringing the white waistcoat to your evening dress if you should want to go to the banquet after the ceremony. And you forgot your razor blades, Professor.

She unpacked, murmuring sounds of worried concern. I didn't listen. Instead I listened to the conversation between MARIANNE *and* EVALD *outside the half-closed door. Their voices were formal and faultlessly polite.*

MARIANNE : No, I'll go tomorrow, so don't worry.

EVALD : Do you intend to stay in a hotel?

MARIANNE *gay* : Why? We can share a bedroom for another night, if you have no objection. Help me to unpack.

EVALD : It was really nice to see you. And unexpected.

MARIANNE : I feel the same way. Are we going to the dinner afterwards, or what do you want to do?

EVALD : I'll just call Stenberg and tell him that I'm bringing a lady. He arranges such things.

> *The door was closed, so I couldn't hear any more of the conversation. I had sat down on the bed to take off my shoes. Miss* AGDA *helped me, but she wasn't very gracious.*

[*Oddly enough, there were three Jubilee Doctors that year. The dean's office had thoughtfully placed us three old men in a special room while the procession was arranged out in the large vestibule of the university hall. I happened to know one of the other two who were going to be honoured. He was an old schoolmate, the former Bishop* JAKOB HOVELIUS. *We greeted each other cordially and embraced. The third old man seemed rather atrophied and declined all conversation. It turned out that he was the former Professor of Roman Law,* CARL-ADAM TIGER (*a great fighter in his time and a man who, according to his students, really lived up to his name*).

ISAK : How comforting it is to meet another old corpse. How are you nowadays, my dear Jakob?

JAKOB : I enjoy my leisure. But don't ask me if I do it *cum dignitate.*

ISAK : Do you know the third man to be honoured?

JAKOB : Of course. It's Carl-Adam Tiger, Professor of Roman Law.

ISAK : The Tiger! Good Lord!

JAKOB : He has three interests left in life. A thirty-year-old injustice, a goldfish, and his bowels.

ISAK : Do you think that we are like that?

JAKOB : What's your opinion? As Schopenhauer says somewhere, ' Dreams are a kind of lunacy and lunacy a kind of dream '. But life is also supposed to be a kind of dream, isn't it? Draw your own conclusion.

ISAK : Do you remember how in our youth we fought with each other on what we called the metaphysical questions?

JAKOB : How could I forget?

ISAK : And what do you believe now?

JAKOB : I'll tell you, I've ceased thinking about all that. One of these days, knowledge will be achieved.

ISAK : My, how surprised you'll be.

JAKOB : And you. But one has a right to be curious.

TIGER : Gentlemen, do you think I'd have time to make a small secret visit before the great farce begins?

ISAK : I don't know, Professor Tiger.

TIGER *sighs*: *In dubio non est agendum*. When in doubt, don't, as the old Romans used to say. I'll stay here.]*

THE FESTIVITIES
What should I describe? Trumpet fanfares, bells ringing, field-cannon salutes, masses of people, the giant procession from the university to the cathedral, the white-dressed garland girls, royalty, old age, wisdom, beautiful music, stately Latin sentences which echoed off the huge vaults. The students and their girls, women in bright, magnificent dresses, this strange rite with its heavy symbolism but as meaningless as a passing dream. Then I saw SARA with her two boys among the onlookers outside the cathedral. They waved to me and suddenly looked childishly happy and full of expectations. Among the lecturers was EVALD, tall and serious, disinterested and absent. Inside the church, I saw MARIANNE in her white dress and next to her sat Miss AGDA, pale and with her lips pressed tightly together. The ceremonial lecture was dull (as usual). The whole

---

* The scene in square brackets does not appear in the finished film.

thing went on endlessly (as usual) and the garland girls had to go out and relieve themselves in the little silver pot in the sacristy. But we adults unfortunately had to stay where we were. As you know, culture provides us with these moments of refined torture. Professor TIGER looked as if he were dying, my friend the BISHOP fell asleep, and more than one of those present seemed ready to faint. Even our behinds, which have withstood long academic services, lectures, dusty dissertations and dull dinners, started to become numb and ache in silent protest. (Stills on page 80 and 97)

I surprised myself by returning to the happenings of the day, and it was then that I decided to recollect and write down everything that had happened. I was beginning to see a remarkable causality in this chain of unexpected, entangled events. At the same time, I couldn't escape recalling the BISHOP's words: ' Dreams are a kind of lunacy and lunacy a kind of dream, but life is also supposed to be a dream, isn't it . . .'

After the ceremony there was a banquet, but I really felt too tired to go. I took a cab home and found Miss AGDA in my room busy making my bed the way I like (very high under my head and folded neatly at my feet). A heating pad was already connected and my sleeping pills stood on the table. Almost at once, Miss AGDA began helping me with my shoes and evening dress, and I felt a great warmth towards this extraordinary, faithful, thoughtful old woman. I would really have liked to become friends with her again, and I repented the morning's thoughtless utterances (which, I noticed, she had by no means forgotten).

ISAK : Did you enjoy the ceremony?

AGDA : Yes, thank you.

ISAK : Are you tired, Miss Agda?

AGDA : I won't deny it.

ISAK : Take one of my sleeping pills.

AGDA : No, thanks.

ISAK : Oh, Miss Agda, I'm sorry for this morning.

AGDA : Are you sick, Professor?

ISAK : No. Why?

AGDA : I don't know, but that sounds alarming.

ISAK : Oh really, is it so unusual for me to ask forgiveness?

AGDA : Do you want the water decanter on the table?

ISAK : No, thanks.

We pottered about for a while, silently.

AGDA : Thanks anyway.

ISAK : Oh, Miss Agda.

AGDA : What do you want, Professor?

ISAK : Don't you think that we who have known each other for two generations could drop formality and say ' *du* ' to each other?

AGDA : No, I don't really think so.

ISAK : Why not, if I may ask?

AGDA : Have you brushed your teeth, Professor?

ISAK : Yes, thanks.

AGDA : Now, I'll tell you. I beg to be excused from all intimacies. It's all right the way it is between us now.

ISAK : But, dear Miss Agda, we are old now.

AGDA : Speak for yourself, Professor. A woman has to think of her reputation, and what would people say if the two of us suddenly started to say ' *du* ' to each other?

ISAK : Yes, what would people say?

AGDA : They would ridicule us.

ISAK : Do you always act correctly?

AGDA : Nearly always. At our age one ought to know how to behave. Isn't that so, Professor?

ISAK : Good night, Miss Agda. *(Still on page 98)*

AGDA : Good night, Professor. I will leave the door ajar. And you know where I am if you should want something. Good night, Professor.

ISAK : Good night, Miss Agda.

I was just going to lie down in bed (I had been sitting on the edge in my old robe) when I heard singing and music from the garden. I thought I recognised the voices and walked over to the window and lifted the blinds. Down there under the trees I recognised my three companions from the trip. They sang to their heart's delight, and ANDERS accompanied them on his guitar.

SARA: Hey, Father Isak! You were fantastic when you marched in the procession. We were real proud that we knew you. Now we're going on.

ANDERS: We got a lift all the way to Hamburg.

VIKTOR: With a fifty-year-old deaconess. Anders is already sweet on the old girl.

ANDERS: Stop babbling!

VIKTOR: We came to say goodbye.

ISAK: Goodbye, and thank you for your company.

SARA: Goodbye, Father Isak. Do you know that it is really you I love, today, tomorrow and forever?

ISAK: I'll remember that.

VIKTOR: Goodbye, Professor.

ISAK: Goodbye, Viktor.

ANDERS: Goodbye, Professor. Now we have to run.

ISAK: Let me hear from you sometime.

> *Those last words I said to myself, and rather quietly. The children waved to me and were swallowed up by the summer night. I heard their laughter, and then they were gone.*
>
> *At the same moment, I heard voices out in the foyer. (Still on page 98) It was* EVALD *and* MARIANNE. *They whispered out of consideration to me and I heard the rustle of* MARIANNE's *evening gown. I called to* EVALD. *He entered the room, but stopped at the door.*

ISAK: Are you home already?

EVALD: Marianne had to change shoes. Her heel broke.

ISAK: So you are going to the dance?

EVALD: Yes, I suppose so.

ISAK: A-ha.

EVALD: How are you otherwise?

ISAK: Fine, thanks.

EVALD: How's the heart holding up?

ISAK: Excellently.

EVALD: Good night, and sleep well.

> *He turned and went through the door. I asked him to come back. He looked very surprised. I felt surprised myself, and confused. I didn't really know what to say.*

ISAK: Sit down a moment.

EVALD : Is it something special?

He sat obediently on the chair near the bed. His starched shirt rustled and his hands hung a little tiredly across his knees. I realised that my son was becoming middle-aged.

ISAK : May I ask you what's going to happen between you and Marianne? EVALD *shakes his head.* Forgive my asking.

EVALD : I know nothing.

ISAK : It's not my business, but . . .

EVALD : What?

ISAK : But shouldn't . . .

EVALD : I have asked her to remain with me.

ISAK : And how will it . . . I mean . . .

EVALD : I can't be without her.

ISAK : You mean you can't live alone.

EVALD : I can't be without *her.* That's what I mean.

ISAK : I understand.

EVALD : It will be as she wants.

ISAK : And if she wants . . . I mean, does she want?

EVALD : She says that she'll think it over. I don't really know.

ISAK : Regarding that loan you had from me . . .

EVALD : Don't worry, you'll get your money.

ISAK : I didn't mean that.

EVALD : You'll get your money all right. *(Still on page 99)*

EVALD rose and nodded to me. Just then MARIANNE appeared in the door. She had on a very simple but extraordinarily beautiful white dress.

MARIANNE : How are you, Father Isak?

ISAK : Fine, thanks. Very well.

MARIANNE : I broke a heel, so we had to come home to change. Can I wear these shoes instead?

ISAK : They look fine.

MARIANNE came up to me. She smelled good and rustled in a sweet, womanly way. She leaned over me.

ISAK : Thanks for your company on the trip. *(Still on page 99)*

MARIANNE : Thank *you.*

ISAK : I like you, Marianne.

MARIANNE : I like you too, Father Isak.

She kissed me lightly on the cheek and disappeared.
They exchanged a few words outside the door. I heard
their steps on the stairs and then the door slamming in
the foyer. I heard my heart and my old watch. I heard
the tower clock strike eleven, with the light tones
designating the four quarter hours and the heavier sounds
marking the hour.
Now it began to rain, not very hard, but quietly and
evenly. A lulling sound. The street lamp swung on its
cord and threw shadows on the light-coloured window
blinds.
Whenever I am restless or sad, I usually try to recall
memories from my childhood, to calm down. This is the
way it was that night too, and I wandered back to the
summerhouse and the wild strawberry patch and every-
thing I had dreamed or remembered or experienced
during this long day.*
I sat under the tree by the wild strawberry patch and
it was a warm, sunny day with soft summer skies and
a mild breeze coming through the birches. Down at the
dock, my sisters and brothers were romping with Uncle
ARON. My aunt went by, together with SARA: They
were laden with large baskets. Everyone laughed and
shouted to each other and applauded when the red sail
went up the mast of the old yacht (an ancient relic from
the days of my parents' childhood; a mad impulse of
our grandfather, the Admiral). SARA turned around and
when she caught sight of me she put down her baskets
and ran towards me. (Still on page 100)

SARA : Isak, darling, there are no wild strawberries left. Aunt
wants you to search for your father. We will sail around the
peninsula and pick you up on the other side. *(Still on page
121)*

ISAK : I have already searched for him, but I can't find

---

* In the film, at the beginning of the dream sequence, the camera dissolves from Isak asleep to the family coming out of the summerhouse
(Still on page 100) and the scene of the family down by the dock
(Still on page 121) appears a little later during the conversation
between Isak and Sara.

either Father or Mother.

SARA : Your mother was supposed to go with him. *(Still on page 122)*

ISAK : Yes, but I can't find them.

SARA : I will help you.

She took me by the hand and suddenly we found our-selves at a narrow sound with deep, dark water. (Still on page 122) The sun shone brightly on the opposite side, which rose softly into a meadow. Down at the beach on the other side of the dark water a gentleman sat, dressed in white with his hat on the back of his head and an old pipe in his mouth. He had a soft, blond beard and pince-nez. He had taken off his shoes and stockings and between his hands he held a long slender bamboo pole. A red float lay motionless on the shimmering water.

Farther up the bank sat my mother. She wore a bright summer dress and a big hat which shaded her face. She was reading a book. (Still on page 123) SARA dropped my hand and pointed to my parents. Then she was gone. (Still on page 123) I looked for a long time at the pair on the other side of the water. I tried to shout to them but not a word came from my mouth. Then my father raised his head and caught sight of me. He lifted his hand and waved, laughing. My mother looked up from her book. She also laughed and nodded.

Then I saw the old yacht with its red sail. It cruised so smoothly in the mild breeze. In the prow stood Uncle ARON, singing some sentimental song, and I saw my brothers and sisters and aunt and SARA, who lifted up SIGBRITT's little boy. I shouted to them, but they didn't hear me.

I dreamed that I stood by the water and shouted towards the bay, but the warm summer breeze carried away my cries and they did not reach their destination. (Still on page 124) Yet I wasn't sorry about that; I felt, on the contrary, rather lighthearted. (Still on page 124)

Stockholm
May 31, 1957

95

WILD STRAWBERRIES

Cutting Continuity

1 Fade in to MS of an old man, Isak, back to camera, sitting at his desk in his study, writing. A gong is heard, off. Isak's voice over. A dog lies on the floor by his chair. *(Still on page 17)*

2 MCU of Isak's head and shoulders, back view; he moves back and pan to reveal his profile in CU. He lights a cigar. Voice over.

3 CU of a large photograph of Evald, his son, next to a small photograph of Evald's wife, Marianne. Slow pan to photograph of them together. Voice over.

4 MCU of a photograph of Isak's mother on a window sill, next to a globe and aneroid barometer. Voice over.

5 CU as Isak's hand picks up a glass of sherry from a silver tray on his desk. Pan up to MCU of him drinking.

6 MCU of a photograph of his wife, Karin, in early middle-age, behind the tray.

7 MS of a door in the study: Agda, his housekeeper appears.

8 MS of Isak turning round to camera. He mutters to her, then voice over. As he rises, track in to CU of his hands tidying the desk.

9 Voice over. MS of Isak standing, back to camera, at his desk. Pan as he moves towards the door, pauses at the chess set, *(Still on page 17)* then signals to his dog. Voice over.

10 MCU of the dog getting up to follow, pan and hold, as it goes off.

11 Low angle MLS of the empty study. Voice over. Fade out.

12 Music over as the credits fade in and out on a black background.

13 CU of Isak asleep, only light on his face. Voice over.

14 Beginning of the dream sequence: CU of Isak in profile, walking through a deserted street, daytime. Slight pan, then hold as he stops; the music stops with him; he turns, walks on into LS.

15 MCU of Isak, back to camera, looking up at a building. He turns and faces camera, then steps back, still looking up.

16 Low angle MCU of a large clock without hands; underneath the optician's sign: a giant model of eyeglasses with broken, staring eyes. *(Still on page 18)*

17 MS of Isak looking up at the blank dial. He takes out his watch.

18 High angle CU of the watch in his hands. The cover clicks open; but the watch has no hands. Sound of heartbeats begins over.

19 MS of Isak closing the watch and looking up. He takes off his hat and puts the watch back in his pocket. As he wipes his forehead, louder sound of his heartbeats. Pan as he walks and stops under the shadow of the clock.

20 Low angle CU of the clock without hands. Heartbeats over.

21 MCU of Isak, then track in to CU. Heartbeats still over.

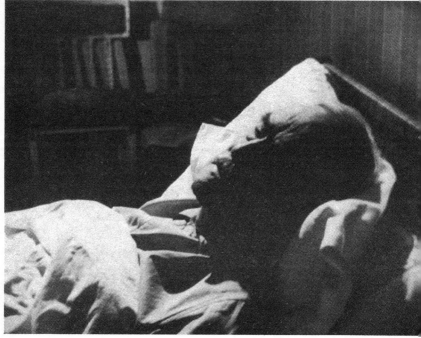

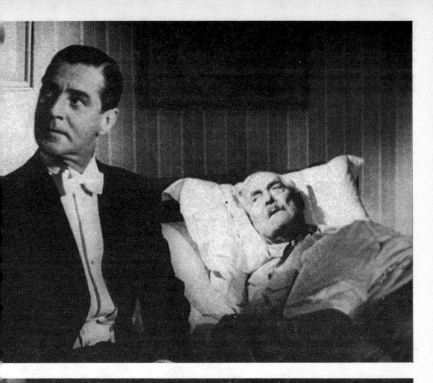

22 LS of Isak on the other side of the deserted street. Track with him as he walks and hold when he stops. He turns round, walks back again faster, camera tracking with him.

23 CU of Isak in profile, then looking towards camera.

24 LS in the other direction, of the deserted street.

25 CU of Isak turning and looking in the opposite direction.

26 LS of a man, back to camera, standing on the street corner.

27 CU of Isak staring, then he begins to move out of shot.

28 MS of Isak, back view, hurrying towards the man; track and hold in MCU as Isak touches his shoulder. *(Still on page 18)* The man turns.

29 CU of Isak, horrified.

30 CU of a grotesque face under a soft felt hat. *(Still on page 18)*

31 CU of Isak, repulsed. *(Still on page 18)*

32 MS of Isak back to camera. The man collapses. *(Still on page 18)*

33 Low angle MCU of Isak looking down. *(Still on page 18)*

34 High angle MCU of the man, exuding a liquid. *(Still on page 18)*

35 MCU of Isak still looking down. He looks up and walks slowly forward, camera tracking with him, until he is in MS, three-quarter back view, looking up the deserted street. Bells toll off.

36 CU of Isak.

37 MLS of another street. A horse-drawn hearse comes round a corner, towards camera.

38 Very LS of Isak standing on the corner of the deserted street, back to camera, as the hearse comes into view round the corner.

39 CU of Isak watching the hearse pass, out of shot.

40 MLS of Isak on the corner. The hearse passes camera from MS into CU going out of shot in foreground. *(Still on page 18)*

41 Low angle MS of the lamp-post, the hearse visible passing it in foreground. The top of the lamp-post wobbles, but does not fall.

42 MCU of Isak watching.

43 High angle CU of the near, inside carriage wheel grinding against the lamp-post. It moves back slightly. *(Still on page 19)*

44 Very low angle MCU of the rear wheel and underside of the carriage moving back. Isak is seen in MLS in background. *(Still on page 19)* Carriage moves forward again, grinding against the lamp-post.

45 Low angle MS of the hearse in the foreground, the lamp-post in background. It grinds and hits the lamp-post again.

46 Very low angle MCU under the carriage. The rear wheel comes loose and rolls towards Isak.

47 Low angle MLS of Isak, the wheel rolling towards him. He dodges *(Still on page 19)* and it crashes against the wall. He looks down.

48 Very low angle MS of the hearse; the horses in CU in foreground. As they move, the hearse rocks and sways. *(Still on page 19)*

49 CU of the hearse by the lamp-post, swaying and teetering.

50 Low angle MS of Isak watching it.

51 Quick low angle MCU of the hearse swaying.

52 Low angle MCU of Isak watching.

53 MCU of the coffin on the swaying hearse.

54 Slight low Angle CU of Isak.

55 MCU of the coffin on the hearse. It shoots forward and slides out.

56 Low angle MLS of the horses bolting into MS, pulling the empty hearse. As it goes out of frame, Isak is seen in LS by the lamp-post.

57 Low angle MLS of Isak, the coffin open on its side in foreground.

58 Reverse shot: high angle MCU of Isak, back view; a corpse's hand sticks out of the coffin, in front of him. *(Still on page 19)*

59 Low angle MS of Isak, staring down.

60 High angle MS of the corpse's hand sticking out of the coffin.

61 Slight low angle CU of Isak.

62 MCU of the hand sticking out of the coffin.

63 CU of the hand in foreground, and Isak in MS background. Isak approaches slowly. *(Still on page 19)* Pan slightly and tilt up as he leans over the coffin.

64 High angle CU of the hand. It rises. Faint, mysterious music fades in over this sequence.

65 Low angle big CU of Isak.

66 Slight high angle CU of the hand moving towards Isak's hand and clutching it. *(Still on page 19)*

67 Low angle CU of Isak wincing, his hand struggling with the dead hand.

68 Big CU of the dead hand gripping Isak's struggling hand.

69 Low angle CU of Isak, pulling back.

70 High angle MCU of the corpse, half visible, pulling itself up.

71 Low angle CU of Isak.

72 High angle CU of the corpse's head moving into full view; it is Isak. *(Still on page 19)*

73 Low angle CU of Isak, horrified, staggering back.

74 High angle CU of the corpse's hand holding onto Isak's wrist.

75 High angle CU of the corpse raising its head.

76 Low angle CU of Isak.

77 High angle CU of the head coming in to extreme CU.

78 Big low angle CU of Isak, trying to free his arm. Music louder.

79 Huge CU of the corpse's face weaving into camera.

80 Large CU of Isak.

81 Large CU of the corpse's eyes and nose so near camera they are out of focus. Zoom in. Music rises, and as it stops, a jump cut to. . . .

82 CU of Isak asleep. Sound of a clock ticking. He turns towards camera and wakes up. Track back as he looks at his watch and gets out of bed. Pan and tilt up as he goes over to the window.

83 MCU of Isak opening the curtains and raising the blind. Daylight. Pan as he goes back to the bed, puts on his robe, and goes through a door.

84 LS of Isak coming through the door into the dining-room. Pan left to right as he crosses the room to another door.
85 MS of Agda in bed. She sits up. *(Still on page 20)*
86 Slight low angle MS of Isak by the door.
87 MS of Agda sitting up, then lying down.
88 MS of Isak going out of the door.
89 MCU of Agda sitting up again, looking after him.
90 MS of Isak standing outside the open door. *(Still on page 20)*
91 MCU of Agda in bed.
92 MS of Isak in the doorway.
93 MCU of Agda in bed.
94 MS of Isak coming through the doorway, then stopping.
95 MCU of Agda, gesturing.
96 MS of Isak in the same position.
97 MCU of Agda lying down again.
98 MS of Isak coming into her room, towards camera.
99 MS of Agda in bed, annoyed.
100 MCU of Isak in the room.
101 MS of Agda sitting up again.
102 MLS of Isak walking away through the door. He stops, turns to camera.
103 MS of Agda getting out of bed. Pan with her as she walks across to a mirror. Hold on her pinning up her hair.
104 LS of Isak in his room, seen through the dining-room door.
105 LS of Agda in her room, seen through the dining-room door.
106 MS of Isak, packing. Agda comes in, takes over, then goes off.
107 MCU of Isak. Pan as he goes to his table. Agda appears in MS.
108 CU of Agda at the door.
109 MS of Isak in foreground, and Agda at the door. She goes out.
110 Dissolve to CU of hands pouring coffee into a cup, with a boiled egg next to it on a table. *(Still on page 20)*
111 MS of Isak sitting at the table, Agda standing, pouring coffee. Agda walks away from camera over to the window.
112 MS of Marianne in her robe, leaning against the doorpost, smoking. *(Still on page 20)*
113 MS of Isak looking towards her, with Agda by the window behind him, watering some flowers. She turns slightly.
114 MS of Marianne at the door.
115 MS of Isak, Agda behind, looking towards Marianne, off.
116 MS of Marianne coming into the room. She flicks ash in ash-tray.
117 MS of Isak, Agda behind. Marianne comes into shot and stands behind him. They talk then she goes off. Agda comes up to Isak.
118 Dissolve to high angle LS of Isak's car driving towards a road junction. Pan with it as it comes up and goes round a square.
119 Dissolve to high angle LS of a road in the country. The car drives towards camera. *(Still on page 20)*
120 MCU seen from the side window, of Isak nearest camera

103

driving, Marianne beside him, talking. He looks at her as she lights a cigarette, then puts it out. He removes his hat; she puts it in the back.

121 Reverse angle MCU of them, from Marianne's side window.

122 Slight low angle MS of the car, from behind, as it drives up a slight gradient into LS.

123 MCU from the side, of Marianne nearest camera, Isak driving.

124 Reverse angle MCU of them, Isak nearest camera.

125 MCU of Marianne, nearest camera, from the side, talking.

126 Reverse angle MCU of Isak, talking.

127 Reverse angle MCU of Marianne, talking.

128 Reverse angle MCU of Isak, talking.

129 Reverse angle MCU of Marianne, talking.

130 CU of Isak full face, seen through the windscreen, driving.

131 MCU of Marianne, seen in profile, looking out of the window.

132 High angle CU, tracking along the road surface, by a white line.

133 MCU of Isak three-quarter front view. Track back and pan to reveal Marianne. Hold on them in MCU, then track and pan in to CU of Marianne. Hold on her, then track and pan to CU of Isak. Hold on him then pan back to CU of Marianne.

134 Very low angle LS tracking forward under the tree tops.

135 CU of Marianne with Isak beside her, both in profile.

136 Reverse angle CU of Isak nearest camera, Marianne in MCU beside him.

137 Dissolve to LS of the car on a country road. It turns off; pan with it from LS into MLS as it disappears behind some trees.

138 MCU of Marianne and Isak in the car facing camera.

139 Dissolve to LS of the car parked in a forest. Marianne and Isak have got out; they shut the doors. Isak walks round the car and joins Marianne. *(Still on page 20)* They come towards camera.

140 Dissolve to LS of them coming round behind a hut in the forest.

141 Dissolve to MS of Marianne and Isak coming up to a tree. *(Still on page 20)* Marianne ducks round a low branch; hold as they stop, and look left, off-screen. Marianne goes out of shot and pan with Isak until he joins her. A house is visible in background. Hold on Isak; Marianne goes off. Faint music over as Isak looks round, first back view, then profile, *(Still on page 20)* then facing camera.

142 MS of Isak, back to camera, looking down. He walks away from camera towards a small tree and kneels down.

143 CU of Isak kneeling and leaning forward. Tilt down with his hand as it touches some wild strawberry leaves. Voice over.

144 MS of Isak leaning down; he sits up facing camera, then looks left at something off-screen. Voice over.

145 MLS of the summer house, its windows boarded up. Voice over.

146 MCU of Isak looking up, towards camera. Voice over.

147 MLS of the summer house as 145. Voice over.

148 Dissolve into MLS of the summer house now bursting with life, windows open and obviously occupied. Voice over.

149 MCU of Isak as 146. Music over. Track in to CU.

150 Dissolve to LS of trees swaying in the breeze. Music louder.

151 Dissolve to low angle LS of the clouds in the summer sky.

152 Dissolve to high angle CU of wild strawberry blossoms. Music.

153 Dissolve to MS of a young girl, in an old-fashioned dress, kneeling in the long grass, picking wild strawberries.

154 MS of Isak watching her. *(Still on page 37)*

155 MS of Sara as 153. *(Still on page 37)* She licks her fingers.

156 MS of Isak leaning further forward, watching her.

157 Quick MS of Sara.

158 CU of Isak's face.*

159 MCU of Sigfrid standing by a tree.

160 MCU of Sara with Sigfrid's legs in shot, behind her.

161 MCU of Sigfrid.

162 MCU of Sara and Sigfrid, same as 160.

163 MLS of Sigfrid standing, Sara kneeling. Sigfrid gets down beside her. Hold in MS, then track in slowly to MCU. Suddenly he kisses her. *(Still on page 37)* She responds passionately, then screams and throws herself to the ground.

164 Jump cut to MCU of Sara, crying. *(Still on page 37)* Pan as she sits up, revealing Sigfrid. Hold in MS then track back. Gong sounds, off. Sara rushes off; hold on Sigfrid with the strawberry basket.

165 LS of the summer house: people running towards it. Gong over.

166 Low angle MS of Benjamin in a tree. Gong still over. He throws his book and straw boater to the ground and jumps. *(Still on page 37)*

167 LS of a sailing boat at a jetty. *(Still on page 37)* Pan left to right to reveal Hagbart hoisting a flag. *(Still on page 37)* Tilt up with the flag almost to the top of the pole. Music in as it rises.

168 MLS of Sigbritt coming from the house and putting her baby into its cradle under a tree near the house.

169 Low angle MS of Anna flinging open a window, shouting.

170 MS of Isak standing up, surprised.

171 LS of the lake, with the grass bank in foreground. The twins appear through the long grass, and shout back to Anna.

172 MCU of Isak as he moves towards camera into CU.

173 MS of Isak, back view, with the summer house in background. He walks through the trees towards the house. Music out.

174 Dissolve to MLS of Isak, coming into a dark corridor in MS. Pan as he passes a staircase and on as he goes to the dining-room door in back view. Track into the room past Isak, revealing Charlotta in MS back view, by a table. Piano plays. Pan as she goes round the table and two boys pass in soft focus. The twins stand by the piano, singing. *(Still on page 37)*

175 MS and fast pan with Isak's aunt, crossing the room, stopping in

---

* End of the first reel.

MLS. Pan as the family assemble at the table. She claps her hands and track in to MS of them. *(Still on page 38)* Pan as they sit down and then across to reveal Isak in the doorway. *(Still on page 38)*

176 MS of Aunt at the head of the table, talking to Benjamin.

177 MS of Benjamin, putting on his napkin.

178 MS of Aunt, tucking in her napkin.

179 MS of Benjamin answering his Aunt.

180 MS of Aunt with Sigbritt passing behind her.

181 MS of Benjamin, talking.

182 MS of Aunt, talking.

183 MS of Hagbart, talking.

184 MS of Aunt, talking.

185 MS of Charlotta, while Aunt speaks, off.

186 MS of Aunt, talking.

187 MS of Benjamin, extending a hand.

188 MS of Uncle Aron, who picks up the basket of strawberries.

189 MS of Sara.

190 MS of Uncle Aron, the strawberry basket in one hand, his ear trumpet in the other. He raises it to his ear.

191 MS of Sara, helping herself to some food.

192 MS of Aunt, talking; the ear trumpet is seen in foreground.

193 MS of Sara, shouting.

194 MS of Sara leaning across Charlotta and shouting into the ear trumpet. *(Still on page 38)* Pan to Uncle Aron, losing the girls.

195 MS of Hagbart, talking.

196 MS of Aunt, talking.

197 MS of the twins, talking in unison.

198 MS of Uncle Aron, talking.

199 MS of Aunt, talking.

200 MS of the twins; they look down and carry on eating.

201 MS of Aunt, talking.

202 MS of the twins, looking up at their Aunt.

203 MS of Aunt, looking at the twins off, then turning towards Anna.

204 MS of Anna bending down under the table. Suddenly, she sits up.

205 MS of Aunt, speaking to Anna.

206 Quick MS of Anna bending down again.

207 MS of Aunt, speaking.

208 MS of Hagbart, Sigfrid, and Benjamin. Sigfrid holds up a picture; the others lean over to look at it. They laugh.

209 MS of the twins, talking in unison.

210 MCU of Sara, shocked.

211 Quick MCU of Sigfrid, the twins talking off.

212 MS of the twins.

213 MS of Sigbritt, talking.

214 MCU of Charlotta, talking.

215 MCU of Benjamin, talking.

216 MCU of Sigfrid pulling off his napkin.

217 MS of Angelica, talking.

218 MCU of Sara; Angelica speaks, off.

219 MCU of Sigfrid.

220 MS of the twins, shrieking and jumping up and down.

221 MCU of Aunt, thunderously telling everyone to be quiet.

222 MS of the twins, silent now and eating.

223 MCU of Sara, throwing her porridge spoon at the twins.

224 MS of the twins, as the spoon crashes onto one of their plates.

225 MCU of Charlotta, amazed at what Sara has done.

226 MCU of Sara, furious. She jumps up, shouting.

227 MLS of the family. Sara's chair falls as she rushes off. Charlotta gets up; pan as she picks up the chair, and goes off after Sara.

228 MCU of Isak standing outside the door. Charlotta comes through towards camera, passing him in MCU. *(Still on page 38)*

229 CU of Sara seen through the bannisters, crying; Charlotta sits behind her in MCU. *(Still on page 38)*

230 CU of Isak looking over the bannisters. Charlotta talks, off.

231 CU of Sara with Charlotta behind her as shot 229.

232 CU of Isak, looking over the bannister rail.

233 CU of Charlotta and Sara. The twins are heard singing, off.

234 CU of Sigfrid conducting, one twin in MCU singing; Hagbart and Benjamin behind. Pan to both twins singing, then pan on losing one twin and revealing Uncle Aron listening through his ear trumpet; Anna behind him. *(Still on page 38)* Pan on to reveal Sigbritt and Aunt. Track back to MS of the family applauding.

235 CU of Isak at the door. He walks towards a door; pan to reveal Sara *(Still on page 38)* then Charlotta. Sara runs through the door, Charlotta goes off. Voice over. Isak goes towards the door.

236 Dissolve to low angle MLS of Sara running, outside the house. Voice over. She comes past camera in MCU as Isak appears in LS.

237 CU of Isak outside the house. Voice over. End of dream sequence.

238 MCU of a blonde girl (Sara, the hitchhiker) leaning on a branch. Pan as she comes and kneels down by Isak who is still sitting near the strawberry patch. Track back slightly to MS of them talking, then she jumps up.

239 High angle MCU of Sara, standing. Isak's head appears in foreground as he gets up. *(Still on page 38)*

240 MS and pan with Marianne as she joins them. Camera holds on them. Marianne and Sara shake hands and they all walk away.

241 Dissolve to high angle MLS of them coming through trees. Pan as Sara runs ahead towards the car, losing Isak and Marianne. Her boyfriends, Anders and Viktor, pop up behind the car; Isak and Marianne come from the left. Hold on them as they exchange greetings and pan with Isak as he goes round the car in MS.

242 Dissolve to CU of Isak driving, with the three hitchhikers in the

back. *(Still on page 39)*
243 CU of Marianne with Viktor sitting behind her.
244 MS of the hitchhikers. Sara takes off her sunglasses and kisses each boy. Track back to reveal Marianne and Isak; Sara leans forward.
245 CU of Isak. Sara comes forward again, and leans on the back of his seat; track back to frame them in MCU; she starts to sit back.
246 Quick cut continuing her movement from the side. Hold in MCU on the hitchhikers. Sara leans forward again.
247 Quick cut continuing her movement from the front, with Isak in MCU driving. She leans on the back of his seat, stroking his cheek.
248 Dissolve to LS of the road ahead seen through the car windscreen. Track forwards with the car until another car is seen in LS, speeding towards them from the opposite direction.
249 CU of Isak startled, the others behind. He swings the wheel.
250 Quick cut to MS of the Volkswagen seen through the car windscreen as it slews off violently, right. *(Still on page 39)*
251 Quick cut to big CU of Marianne bracing herself.
252 Quick cut to MLS of the Volkswagen skidding.
253 Quick CU of Isak, startled.
254 MS from Isak's point of view, looking through the windscreen and across the bonnet, as his car skids off the road.
255 CU of Sara protecting her head, Anders and Viktor beside her.
256 LS of the Volkswagen skidding and rolling over onto its roof.
257 CU of the front of Isak's car, coming towards camera.
258 Big CU of Sara screaming and throwing herself back.
259 CU of the front bumper and wing of Isak's car, stopping.
260 LS of the Volkswagen which has rolled further over.
261 MCU through the side window of Anders and Sara getting up. Pan to Isak and Marianne, looking round. Isak starts to get out.
262 LS of them all by Isak's car; they run towards camera into MLS.
263 LS of the Volkswagen: a couple get out and run towards camera.
264 MLS of the hitchhikers with Isak and Marianne behind them.
265 MLS of Alman, with his wife Berit, standing near their car.
266 MLS, same as 264.
267 High angle MS, over Viktor's shoulder, of Alman with Berit behind. Pan as Alman comes up to Anders, losing Viktor and Berit, revealing Sara behind Anders; pan as he goes towards Sara, Marianne and Isak.
268 High angle MS of Berit, curtseying. She comes towards camera; pan to include Alman in the shot.
269 MS of Isak and Marianne with Sara behind.
270 MCU of Alman and Berit with Anders behind.
271 MS as 269. Pan with Isak walking past Berit and Alman; hold, then Alman goes off; Marianne in LS goes towards Isak's car.
272 High angle MS of Sara, Viktor and Anders, trying to get the Volkswagen upright. Alman comes into shot and helps them.

273 Reverse MS of Isak with Berit behind him, fixing a rope to the bumper of the Volkswagen. Alman's hand is visible in foreground. Isak's car, driven by Marianne, backs into shot in background.

274 MS of the four pushing the Volkswagen. *(Still on page 40)*

275 MS of Berit behind Isak.

276 MS of Alman pushing the Volkswagen, which is almost upright. As the car lands, the others are revealed. Hold as Viktor walks off, and Anders steers the car, through the window.

277 MS of Marianne fixing a rope to the back bumper of Isak's car. *(Still on page 40)* Pan as she runs round it, gets in, and drives off.

278 MS of the group round the Volkswagen which is being towed onto the road. Pan then hold in MS. *(Still on page 57)* Pan as the car moves off: Anders is steering, Alman giving orders.

279 High angle MCU of Viktor undoing the tow rope and going off. The Volkswagen drives into full CU.

280 MS of the group from behind; Sara and Anders pushing the Volkswagen, Alman driving it into LS. It stops.

281 MCU of Isak with Berit, smiling; Isak goes off.

282 Dissolve to CU of Isak in his car, Alman behind him. Pan to Marianne driving, Berit behind, Sara behind Berit.

283 MCU of Viktor, Sara with a pipe, and Anders, in the back seat.

284 MS seen from the side, of Berit and Alman, sitting on folding seats, with Sara and Anders visible behind.

285 MCU of Marianne with Berit and Alman behind. The hitchhikers visible at the back. *(Still on page 57)*

286 MCU of Isak looking out of the window. *(Still on page 58)*

287 MCU of Alman and Berit, with the hitchhikers behind them.

288 MCU of Berit. She slaps Alman who is off-screen. Track into CU of her hitting him; pan to Alman protecting his face with his hand; pan back to Berit, shouting.*

289 LS of the car driving along the road away from camera.

290 CU of Marianne from the side: she has stopped the car.

291 MCU over Isak's shoulder, of Alman and Berit. Alman gets out and Berit follows. The three hitchhikers watch them go.

292 LS of the car, Alman and Berit beside it. It drives off and they watch it go, then slowly walk after it, away from camera.

293 High angle LS of the car driving into MS; pan as it passes.

294 High angle MS of the car passing. Voice over. Tilt up as the car drives into LS: a lake and hills are seen.

295 High angle MS of the car driving, the lake in the distance. Pan as it goes into a garage forecourt. It stops. Voice still over.

296 MS of Akerman, coming out of his office. Pan as he comes round a car towards camera. Track back as he comes into MCU, and pan as he goes up to the window of Isak's car. They are all getting out.

---

* End of reel 2.

297 Low angle MLS of Eva, Akerman's wife, washing a car in the garage; she stops and walks towards camera.

298 MS of Isak and Akerman by some petrol pumps. Eva comes up to them. Hold, then Akerman moves along to the bonnet.

299 MS of Akerman at the bonnet. He opens it and Isak comes into shot, followed by Eva. As they talk, Akerman attends to the car.

300 MS of Akerman with Isak and Eva behind him.

301 MCU of Marianne, now back in the car, seen through the window.

302 MCU of Isak then track back to include Akerman.

303 MS of Akerman, Isak in the centre, and Eva. They shake hands.

304 High angle MS of the car. Isak walks round it towards camera; pan as he gets in; the hitchhikers also get in. The car drives off.

305 Dissolve to high angle LS looking towards Lake Vättern. Tilt down to high angle MS of them all having lunch on an open terrace. Laughter against Isak's voice over. *(Still on page 58)*

306 MS of the group, Isak at the end, Marianne and Sara each side of him, Viktor and Anders nearest camera. Voice over.

307 MS of Marianne and Isak; she lights his cigar.

308 MS of Sara and Anders with Viktor in foreground, back view.

309 MS of Viktor.

310 MS, same as 308.

311 MS of Viktor.

312 MS, same as 308.

313 MS of Viktor.

314 MS of Anders.

315 MS of Viktor.

316 MS of Anders.

317 MS of Viktor.

318 MS of Anders.

319 MS of Viktor, drinking.

320 MS of Isak and Sara.

321 MS of Viktor.

322 MS of Anders, pouring wine into his glass.

323 MS of Viktor.

324 MS of Anders.

325 MS of Isak and Sara.

326 MS of the group, looking along the table to Isak at the end.

327 MCU of Isak with the lake behind him.

328 MS of Viktor and Marianne, from Isak's point of view.

329 MS of Sara and Anders.

330 MS of Viktor and Marianne.

331 MCU of Isak. As he speaks, music slowly comes in. He drinks.

332 MS of Viktor and Marianne. Music out.

333 MS of Sara and Anders.

334 MS of Marianne in profile, looking towards Isak, full face.

335 High angle MS of the group. Marianne and Isak leave.

336 Dissolve to LS of an old house surrounded by trees. Marianne and Isak are seen going towards the front door.

337 MS, panning with them, as they go up the steps.

338 Dissolve to MCU of a nurse, back view, opening a door, revealing Isak in MS. He comes through it towards camera as the nurse goes off. Isak comes into CU and goes off. Marianne walks into CU. The nurse crosses frame and goes back through the door; hold on Marianne.

339 MLS of Isak standing by his mother, who sits at a large desk.

340 High angle MCU of his mother; Isak bending over her.

341 MS and pan as Marianne comes to join Isak and his mother who extends her hand. Marianne curtsies. *(Still on page 59)*

342 High angle MCU of Isak's mother; his arm visible on the left.

343 MS of Marianne, Isak, and his mother. Marianne goes out of shot.

344 High angle CU of a box carried by Marianne. Pan as she places it on the desk in MCU back view, and moves away revealing Isak and his mother. Pan on picking her up as she removes the lid.

345 MCU of Isak then tilt down to his mother; Isak partly visible in foreground. Track back to MS of them looking at the open box.

346 CU of Isak and his mother; she takes out a book.

347 Slight low angle MCU of Marianne.

348 High angle CU of his mother's hands lifting an old china doll from the box. *(Still on page 59)* Tilt up to MCU of her holding the doll. *(Still on page 59)* Pan as she hands it to Marianne.

349 High angle CU of the contents of the box including a photograph.

350 MCU of Marianne still holding the doll.

351 Slight high angle MCU of his mother's hands holding an old painting book. Pan to MCU of her in profile, then facing.

352 MCU of Isak in profile, holding a toy train; track in to CU.

353 MCU of Isak's mother with Isak in foreground.

354 MCU of Marianne.

355 MS of Isak and his mother.

356 High angle CU of his mother's hands holding a box; she opens it, revealing a gold watch without hands. Drum beats in. Tilt up slightly with her hands as the watch comes into CU.

357 CU of Isak. Drum beats over.

358 CU of the gold watch without hands. Drum beats rise as camera tracks into big CU. *(Still on page 59)*

359 CU of Isak as the drum beats fade out. *(Still on page 59)*

360 CU of his mother and tilt up to Isak. Music in and out. Pan down to include his mother as he kisses her on the forehead. *(Still on page 59)* Isak goes out of shot.

361 MCU of Marianne still holding the doll. She puts it down.

362 Dissolve to MCU of Sara by the car. *(Still on page 59)*

363 Slight low angle MLS of Marianne, Isak and Sara by the car. Sara and Isak get inside and Marianne helps him.

364 Slight high angle MCU of Isak in the car seen through the side

window. Pan to MS of Sara behind with Marianne outside, looking in the back side-window. Pan to re-frame Sara, then on as she leans on Isak's seat in MCU. Marianne is seen outside.

365 LS of Anders and Viktor fighting in the long grass.

366 MCU of Isak and Sara inside, Marianne outside. She walks off.

367 Slight low angle MLS of Anders and Viktor fighting near the car. Marianne between them, manages to part them. *(Still on page 59)*

368 MS of Sara sitting in the back of the car. Viktor in CU, gets in and as he sits back and closes the door, Anders is revealed.

369 Dissolve to high angle LS of the sea and sky. Thunder is heard.

370 Dissolve to MLS of the road seen through the windscreen and moving windscreen wipers. Music from Anders' guitar, off.

371 Slight low angle MS from the side, of Anders furthest from camera playing his guitar; Sara and Viktor nearest camera.

372 MCU of Marianne driving, with Isak next to her. Voice over. Camera tracks in to CU of Isak. Dream sequence begins.

373 Dissolve to low angle LS of a flock of large birds circling in the dark sky. Noise of birds screeching. *(Still on page 60)*

374 Dissolve to low angle LS of large birds flying among tree tops.

375 Dissolve to high angle CU of the basket of wild strawberries spilled on the grass. *(Still on page 60)*

376 Dissolve to slight high angle MS of Cousin Sara front view, Isak three-quarter back view, sitting down. Summer house in background.

377 MCU of Sara back view and Isak front view; she holds up a mirror.

378 Reverse angle MCU of Sara and Isak; his face visible in the mirror which Sara is holding. *(Still on page 60)*

379 Reverse angle MCU of them, favouring Isak.

380 Reverse angle MCU of them, favouring Sara.

381 Reverse angle MCU of them, favouring Isak.

382 Reverse angle MCU of them, favouring Sara.

383 MCU, favouring Isak; Sara, back view, holding up the mirror.

384 MCU of Sara holding the mirror with Isak's face visible in it.

385 CU of Isak with the light of the mirror, reflected on his face.

386 MCU of Sara.

387 CU of Isak.

388 MCU of Sara.

389 CU of Isak.

390 MS of Sara front view, Isak back view, sitting on the ground with the summer house in the background. Sara gets up. Music in. Pan as she runs off into the forest. Noise of screeching birds.

391 LS of Sara running towards camera through the forest. Pan and track with her as she runs along in MLS.

392 MLS of the arbour and Sigbritt's baby's cradle. Noise of the baby crying and the screeching birds. Sara runs into shot towards the cradle. She bends over it. *(Still on page 60)*

112

393 MCU of Sara holding the baby. Track in. *(Still on page 60)*
394 MLS of the cradle and the arbour. Pan with Sara holding the baby as she runs towards the house, where someone waits at a door.
395 Low angle LS of the birds, flying around in the dark sky.
396 MS of the cradle under the arbour, silhouetted against the sky. Isak appears and looks at it. Music; birds screeching.
397 Slight high angle CU of Isak. He looks up; tilt up to the claw-shaped branches of the tree, silhouetted against the dark sky.
398 Dissolve from the branch to MCU of Isak approaching the house. Track back with him. As the music ends a piano is heard playing.
399 CU of Isak's back. He walks on and stops at a window in MS. Pan as he walks by the dark wall to another window. Track in to MCU.
400 MS, seen through the window, of Sara in evening dress, playing a piano; Sigfrid standing beside her. He kisses her neck and as they embrace, she stops playing. Violin music in. *(Still on page 60)* Pan as they go into MLS and sit at a table. Track back to reveal the dark windows with the sky reflected on them. Violin music out.
401 LS of the moon appearing from behind the trees.
402 Slight low angle MCU of Isak looking up; pan as he turns away from camera and looks through the dark window. He raps on it; track and pan slightly to CU of his other hand on the window frame. He moves it away revealing a nail; pan back to him looking at his cut palm, back to camera, his reflection on the window pane. The moon is reflected on the window pane next to him. He moves away from the window and Alman, inside, peers through at him in CU. He opens the window towards camera, Isak goes through into the house.
403 MLS of Alman and Isak in an empty room, moonlight streaming through the windows as they come into MS. Track back slightly as they go into a hall and Isak takes off his coat; pan slightly as they walk away from camera and into a door on the other side of the hall.*
404 MS of an empty corridor lit by wall lamps. Footsteps, off. Alman and Isak appear in LS, walking towards camera. Alman stops and unlocks a door in MS and goes in; hold on Isak by the open door.
405 MCU of Isak by the door. Camera zooms in to CU.
406 MCU of Alman in the room, back to camera; Isak by the door facing him in MS. He comes into the room, Alman goes to close the door.
407 MLS of the room: a lecture theatre. About ten people are seated in the benches, among them Sara, Anders and Viktor.
408 MCU of Alman and Isak by the door. Alman closes it and passes in front of Isak, going out of shot. Isak looks round, then follows.
409 MS of a desk in front of a blackboard. Alman sits down behind

---

* End of reel 3.

it and Isak sits down in front of it nearest camera, back view. *(Still on page 60)* Hold as Alman leafs through some papers and Isak passes him a small book. Isak rises.

410 CU of Isak looking into a microscope on Alman's desk.

411 Very big CU of an eye.

412 CU of Isak by the microscope. Alman appears and looks in to it. Pan as Isak sits down; the microscope in foreground. *(Still on page 60)*

413 Slight low angle MCU of Alman in front of the blackboard. He turns away then moves out of shot; camera holds on blackboard.

414 High angle MCU of Isak, looking up at the blackboard.

415 MCU of Alman turning away from the blackboard, towards camera.

416 MCU, of Isak same as 414.

417 Low angle MCU of Alman.

418 MCU of Isak, same as 414.

419 MCU of Alman, same as 417.

420 MCU of Isak, same as 414.

421 MCU of Alman, same as 417.

422 MCU of Isak, same as 414.

423 MCU of Alman, same as 417.

424 MCU of Isak, same as 414.

425 Low angle CU of Alman, leaning forward. *(Still on page 77)*

426 MCU of Isak, microscope in foreground. He laughs and turns to look at the audience. Pan slightly to reveal them sitting in the benches in LS. Isak looks at them, then turns back slowly.

427 MCU of Alman from the side. Pan, revealing Isak, and pan on, losing Alman, then back to both Alman and Isak. *(Still on page 77)*

428 CU of a water decanter and glasses on a tray. Isak's hand comes forward. Tilt up and pan to MCU of Isak pouring water into a glass. *(Still on page 77)* Pan to low angle MCU of Alman. He gets up and pan with him to include Isak. Alman goes out of shot.

429 Low angle MCU of Alman turning on a bright light. He adjusts it and Isak appears in front of him, and bends down.

430 High angle CU of the top of Berit's head. Isak's hand lifts her face. Tilt up to include him in CU. *(Still on page 77)* She seems dead, but suddenly laughs. Tilt up further to Isak.

431 MS of Alman three-quarter back view writing at the desk. Isak appears and Alman turns towards him, reading something. Track into CU of them both: Alman crosses frame and goes over to the door in MS, soft focus; Isak pauses, then turns towards him. Music in as Alman goes out of the door and Isak follows him.

432 Dissolve to high angle CU of their reflections on a pond. Pan as their reflections move across the water. Music louder. Tilt up to MS of Alman followed by Isak going into a clearing in a forest.

433 Dissolve to MS of Isak following Alman through the forest. They walk towards a hut in MLS.

114

434 MS of Isak coming past the hut. Alman follows. Track in to MCU. Music out.

435 LS of a clearing in the forest.

436 CU of Isak with Alman in MCU behind him. A woman's laughter, off.

437 LS of the clearing. A man and a woman appear together.

438 MS of them both. He leans over and kisses her. She laughs and turns towards camera; track in to MCU as she looks in a mirror.

439 MCU of Isak in the trees, watching them.

440 MCU of the woman; the man's hand takes out the pins in her hair. She pushes him and goes off. Pan to MCU of the man.

441 MS of the woman as the man's arms come into shot and grab her. Pan as he pulls her towards him, until they are framed in MCU. She struggles violently. *(Still on page 77)* Track in to CU as he pushes her onto the ground, struggling, fighting, and hitting out at him.

442 MS of Isak with Alman behind him.

443 LS of the man and woman in the clearing; she runs round, laughing.

444 MCU of the woman.

445 MCU of the man.

446 MCU of the woman.

447 MCU of the man, as he starts to walk towards her.

448 MCU of the woman, as she walks towards him.

449 Quick high angle MS of the woman, falling to her knees.

450 MCU of Isak and Alman. *(Still on page 77)* Zoom in to CU.

451 MCU of the woman kneeling, her head and shoulders visible. The man's hand appears and grabs her hair. *(Still on page 77)* Tilt up with her head, being gripped by his hand, framing them in MCU. Pan across and down as she pulls him down onto her. *(Still on page 77)*

452 LS of the clearing: the couple just visible on the ground.

453 MS of Isak and Alman, watching.

454 MS of the woman sitting on the ground, adjusting her skirt.

455 MS of the man sitting on a log.

456 CU of Isak, watching.

457 Slight high angle CU of the woman, looking in a mirror.

458 CU of Isak, watching.

459 CU of the woman, same as 457. She pins up her hair.

460 CU of Isak, same as 458.

461 CU of the woman, same as 457.

462 LS of the clearing: the woman stands up and moves away into the trees, the man goes in the opposite direction.

463 MS of Isak and Alman. Isak moves forward. Zoom into CU of him.

464 Quick LS of the clearing.

465 CU of Isak looking back towards Alman, out of shot.

466 CU of Alman moving forward. Track back to frame Alman and

Isak in MCU. Music in, as camera slowly tracks in to CU of Isak.
467 Slow dissolve to MCU of Isak, asleep in the car. As he wakes up,
the music get louder; pan to Marianne sitting in the driving seat. Music
over. Track back slightly to MCU of them both, from the side.
468 MLS of Anders, Sara and Viktor, picking flowers in the hedgerow.
469 MS of Isak and Marianne in the car, talking.
470 MCU of Marianne from Isak's point of view.
471 MCU of Isak, from Marianne's point of view.
472 MCU of Marianne, same as 470.
473 MCU of Isak.
474 MCU of Marianne.
475 MCU of Isak.
476 MCU of Marianne.
477 MCU of Isak.
478 MCU of Marianne, then track in to CU.
479 Flash back: MCU of Evald in a car. Track back to reveal
Marianne nearest camera in profile. *(Still on page 78)*
480 MCU of Evald nearest camera, Marianne sitting next to him.
481 MCU of them both, Marianne nearest camera.
482 MCU of Evald and Marianne, same as 480.
483 MCU, same as 481. Evald gets out of the car, and slams the door.
Camera pans slightly across and holds on Marianne.
484 MCU of Marianne, seen from Evald's window; she gets out.
485 Slight low angle MCU of Evald, back to camera, standing in the
rain by a dead tree. Marianne comes up and stands beside him in profile.
He turns towards camera and goes off. Hold on Marianne in MCU.
486 Slight low angle MCU of Evald, looking at her, off.
487 MCU of Marianne, by the dead tree.
488 MCU of Evald.
489 MS of Evald getting into the car, seen through the side window.
490 MCU of Evald nearest camera, Marianne gets in beside him.
491 MCU of them both, Marianne nearest camera. Track in to CU
of Evald. End of flash back.
492 CU of Marianne in Isak's car; track back to reveal Isak sitting
next to her, nearest camera. She lights a cigarette.
493 MCU of Isak, with Marianne nearest camera. *(Still on page 78)*
494 MCU of Isak and Marianne, front view. Track and pan to MCU
of Isak, losing Marianne, and revealing by the window, the three
hitchhikers, holding a bouquet of flowers, singing. *(Still on page 79)*
Sara passes the bouquet through the window to Isak and he places
it on his lap. Track in to CU of him. Music out as the background
gets dark.
495 Dissolve to low angle LS of the towers of a church. Pan across
and down to reveal the car driving towards camera past houses in LS.
496 Dissolve to MLS of white gates: Isak stands behind them with
Sara, Anders and Viktor. Isak comes through the gates, the others

go off.

497 MS and pan with Agda, running along a path. Isak appears, gives her the flowers and they exchange greetings. Anders appears with Isak's suitcase and she takes it from him.

498 MCU of Marianne at the boot of the car, Anders behind her.

499 MS of Agda, facing camera and Isak, back view, on the foot path.

500 MS, panning with Evald as he walks through the foyer of his house. Hold as Isak comes in, followed by Marianne. Evald walks up to greet them. Track back to frame all three in MS. The others come in behind. *(Still on page 79)* Pan as they move towards the stairs.

501 High angle MLS of Evald, Marianne and Isak, coming up the stairs. Track back as they climb, and hold outside a door. Agda appears, takes Isak's case and walks off. Isak follows; pan after him.

502 MS of Agda and Isak coming into the guest room. Isak comes towards camera and sits down.

503 MS of a half-open door in the room. Evald is just visible behind it. The door swings open to reveal Marianne and Evald in MLS.*

504 MCU of Isak, with Agda bending over him, in the bedroom.

505 Dissolve to the Festivities: low angle LS of trumpeters on a balcony of a large building.

506 Low angle LS of one of the church towers, seen through the trees.

507 MS of part of the procession coming through a door, followed by Isak and two other men. *(Still on page 80)*

508 MLS of the procession; the trumpeters just visible top of frame.

509 Low angle MCU of Evald in the procession. *(Still on page 97)*

510 Low angle MS of Isak, with other men coming down some steps. Isak stops and looks to the left for a moment.

511 High angle MS of a crowd of people with Sara, Viktor and Anders in the foreground, waving. *(Still on page 97)*

512 MS of Isak smiling at them, as he goes down the steps past camera.

513 MLS of the procession going along the road lined with crowds.

514 MS of the head of the procession coming towards camera.

515 Dissolve to low angle MS of a man standing near a stained glass window in the cathedral. He turns away from camera and begins to conduct. Bells ring as the trumpet fanfare ends. Music in.

516 MLS of the audience: Agda and Marianne in front. They all stand up.

517 High angle MLS of the procession coming down the aisle. *(Still on page 97)*

518 MCU of the audience, same as 516.

519 MLS, same as 517. The procession coming further towards camera and moving out of shot at bottom of frame.

520 MCU of Agda and Marianne; others behind them. *(Still on page 97)*

---

* End of reel 4.

521 Low angle MS of the ceremonial lecturer, on a dais, delivering his speech. He puts on his own hat. *(Still on page 97)*
522 MS of the soldiers outside, with two cannons firing salutes. *(Still on page 97)*
523 MCU of Isak looking down. He looks up; rises. *(Still on page 97)*
524 Slight high angle MS of Agda and Marianne in the audience.
525 MS of Isak going up to the ceremonial lecturer to receive his honorary doctorate. The lecturer places the ceremonial hat on Isak's head. *(Still on page 97)* Music in as Isak's voice over. He places the ring on Isak's finger and gives him the scroll. They shake hands and bow; pan as Isak comes up onto the dais. They shake hands again, and Isak crosses and steps down on the other side; they bow again. Pan further as an usher helps Isak over to his seat. He bows to someone off screen.
526 Slight low angle MCU of Isak bowing; the usher behind him. He turns and bows towards camera. Music out.
527 Dissolve to CU of Agda's hand putting out some pills, Isak's hand holding a glass of water. His hand picks up a pill.
528 MS of Agda, with Isak sitting on the bed taking the pills. Agda goes over to the mantelpiece and puts down the glass. Pan with her as she puts out the light, opens the window, and draws the curtains. Pan back as she goes over to the door and turns towards Isak.
529 MS of Isak sitting on his bed.
530 MCU of Agda at the door.
531 Slight high angle MCU of Isak facing camera.
532 Slight low angle MCU of Agda.
533 MCU of Isak, same as 531.
534 MCU of Agda, same as 532.
535 MCU of Isak, same as 531.
536 MS, panning with Agda as she comes over to Isak. *(Still on page 98)* Pan back with her as she goes over to the door.
537 MCU of Agda standing at the door.
538 Slight high angle MS of Isak three-quarters back to camera, sitting on the bed. As he turns out the bedside light, singing is heard, off. He gets up; pan with him as he goes over to the window.
539 MS of Isak coming through the French windows onto a balcony.
540 Very high angle MLS, from Isak's point of view, of Anders, Viktor and Sara in the garden, serenading him.
541 Slight low angle MCU of Isak on the balcony, looking down.
542 High angle MLS of the hitchhikers, same as 540.
543 MCU of Isak, same as 541.
544 High angle MLS of Sara in the garden, looking up towards Isak.
545 MCU of Isak, same as 541.
546 High angle MLS of Sara, same as 544.
547 MCU of Isak, same as 541.
548 High angle MLS of Sara. The boys appear, trying to drag her off.

549 MCU of Isak, same as 541.

550 High angle LS of Sara, Anders and Viktor; tilt up as they run off into LS through the gates.

551 MCU of Isak on the balcony, watching them go. Bells chime, off.

552 Dissolve to MCU of Isak asleep. *(Still on page 98)* He stirs.

553 MS of the door ajar: Marianne visible outside it. It closes.

554 MCU of Isak, same as 552, but now he is awake.

555 MS of Evald opening the door.

556 High angle MS of Isak lying in bed.

557 MS of Evald, standing by the door.

558 High angle MS of Isak in bed.

559 MS of Evald, same as 557.

560 High angle MS of Isak in bed, same as 558.

561 MS of Evald, same as 557.

562 High angle MS of Isak in bed, same as 558.

563 MS of Evald, same as 557. He turns to go.

564 High angle MS of Isak in bed, same as 558.

565 LS of Evald at the door, Isak in bed in the foreground. Evald comes towards camera and sits down by Isak's bed in MS.

566 MS of Evald sitting with Isak lying in bed. *(Still on page 99)*

567 LS of Marianne at the door, Evald and Isak in foreground. Evald gets up and Marianne comes over to Isak, who leans forward. She bends down to kiss him as Evald goes out in LS.

568 MCU of Marianne and Isak. Hold as they talk. She kisses him goodnight, *(Still on page 99)* gets up and leaves.

569 High angle MCU of Isak lying in bed. Voice over. Camera tracks in to high angle CU. Music in and out.

570 Beginning of dream sequence: dissolve to LS of the summer house with a group of children coming out. *(Still on page 100)* Cousin Sara runs towards camera into MS.

571 Slight high angle MS of Isak standing by the trees.

572 MS of Sara coming towards him. *(Still on page 100)*

573 MS of Sara and Isak, standing by the trees. *(Still on page 121)*

574 High angle MLS of the family getting into the sailing boat. A boy is pushed into the water by the twins. *(Still on page 121)*

575 MS of Sara and Isak by the trees, watching. *(Still on page 122)* They walk away from camera.

576 Dissolve to MLS of Sara leading Isak through a meadow of seeding grasses, with tall trees behind. Music in and out.

577 Dissolve to low angle MS of Sara leading Isak among the trees. *(Still on page 122)* Coming towards camera, Sara points.

578 LS of Isak's mother and father on the other side of the lake. His father is fishing and his mother sits behind him on a rug knitting. *(Still on page 123)* Hold, then they wave to Isak.

579 Low angle MS of Sara and Isak, watching. Sara runs off, leaving Isak standing alone. *(Still on page 123)*

580 LS of his mother and father, sitting on the bank. Music in and out.
581 Low angle CU of Isak. *(Still on page 124)* Music in and out.
Camera tracks in slowly to big CU.
582 Very slow dissolve (music in and out) to high angle CU of Isak's
head on the pillow. *(Still on page 124)* He wakes up and then
settles back to sleep. Music in and out. Fade to black.*

----

* End of reel 5.

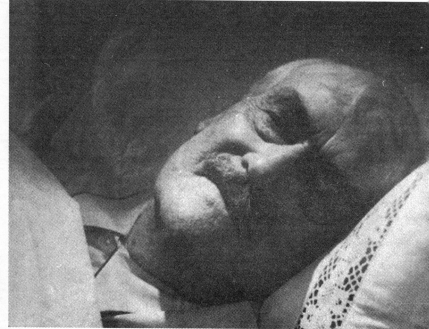